Edexcel GCSE

History
Controlled Assessment
CA1 Germany 1918–39

John Child and Rob Bircher
Series editor: Angela Leonard

Introduction

This topic is a fascinating study of how fragile democracy can be.

First, we see how, at the end of the First World War, the German emperor fled. In his place, the German people created a brand new democratic state – the Weimar Republic. It gave more Germans the vote and allowed them to elect their own president, chancellor (government leader) and parliament. But we also see how the Weimar Republic struggled to establish itself, and how it never really had the full support of the German people. Although it had a period of stability in the middle of the 1920s, once it hit the economic rocks in 1929, it quickly fell apart. We see how the popular leader of the Nazis, Adolf Hitler, developed his party and gained the support of enough voters to become the new chancellor in 1933.

Hitler never really believed in democracy, so the rest of the unit shows how he and the Nazis dismantled the democratic state and changed German society. We see how they changed the lives of young people, women and workers; we see how they turned Germany into a police state; we see how they used the power of the state to control the minds of the people and how they used this power against the Jews and other minorities. It's a chilling story about how democracy can go wrong.

Part A of this book covers:

- the Weimar Republic 1918–32
- Hitler and the growth of the Nazi Party 1918–33
- the Nazi dictatorship 1933–39
- key features of Nazi rule 1933–39.

For your controlled assessment in this unit, you will learn how to carry out an enquiry (Part A) and how to analyse and evaluate representations of history (Part B). Later sections of this book cover the skills you will need to be successful in unit 4.

Your Part A enquiry will focus in detail on one key question. In Part B you will focus on representations of history: how to analyse, compare and evaluate different views of how the Nazis were able to control Germany.

Contents

Germany 1918–39

Part A: Carry out a historical enquiry
- A1 The Weimar Republic 1918–32 4
- A2 Hitler and the growth of the Nazi Party 1918–33 14
- A3 The Nazi dictatorship 1933–39 26
- A4 Key features of Nazi rule 1933–39 36
- Enquiry and writing skills support 44

Part B: Representations of history
- How were the Nazis able to control Germany 1933–39? 54
- Understanding and analysing representations of history 60
- Evaluating representations 67

ResultsPlus Maximise your marks 72
Glossary 79

Part A: Carry out a historical enquiry

Part A Carry out a historical enquiry

A1 The Weimar Republic 1918–32

> **Learning outcomes**
> By the end of this topic, you should be able to:
> - picture an overview of the history of the Weimar Republic 1918–32
> - analyse its difficulties 1918–23
> - explain its recovery 1924–29
> - understand its problems 1929–32

1. By November 1918, Germany was losing the First World War. Sailors at the naval port of Kiel mutinied and there were strikes and riots in many cities. With his country in rebellion, Kaiser Wilhelm fled abroad. Germany became a democratic republic, soon named the Weimar Republic. Its history after 1918 was a real rollercoaster ride.

2. 1918–1923 were difficult years for the new republic. There were several attempts to overthrow the government, such as the Spartacus Revolt (1919), the Kapp Putsch (1920) and the Munich Putsch (1923). This political unrest was partly caused by terrible economic problems – government debts, huge debt repayments and, in 1923, serious inflation.

3. From late 1923 to 1929, the Weimar Republic enjoyed a revival. This was partly because of the Weimar Republic's most successful minister, Gustav Stresemann.
He solved the problem of inflation in 1923. He also helped to seal deals which reduced Germany's debt repayments. These were called the Dawes Plan (1924) and Young Plan (1929). He also regained German pride in international affairs, for example getting Germany accepted into the League of Nations in 1926.

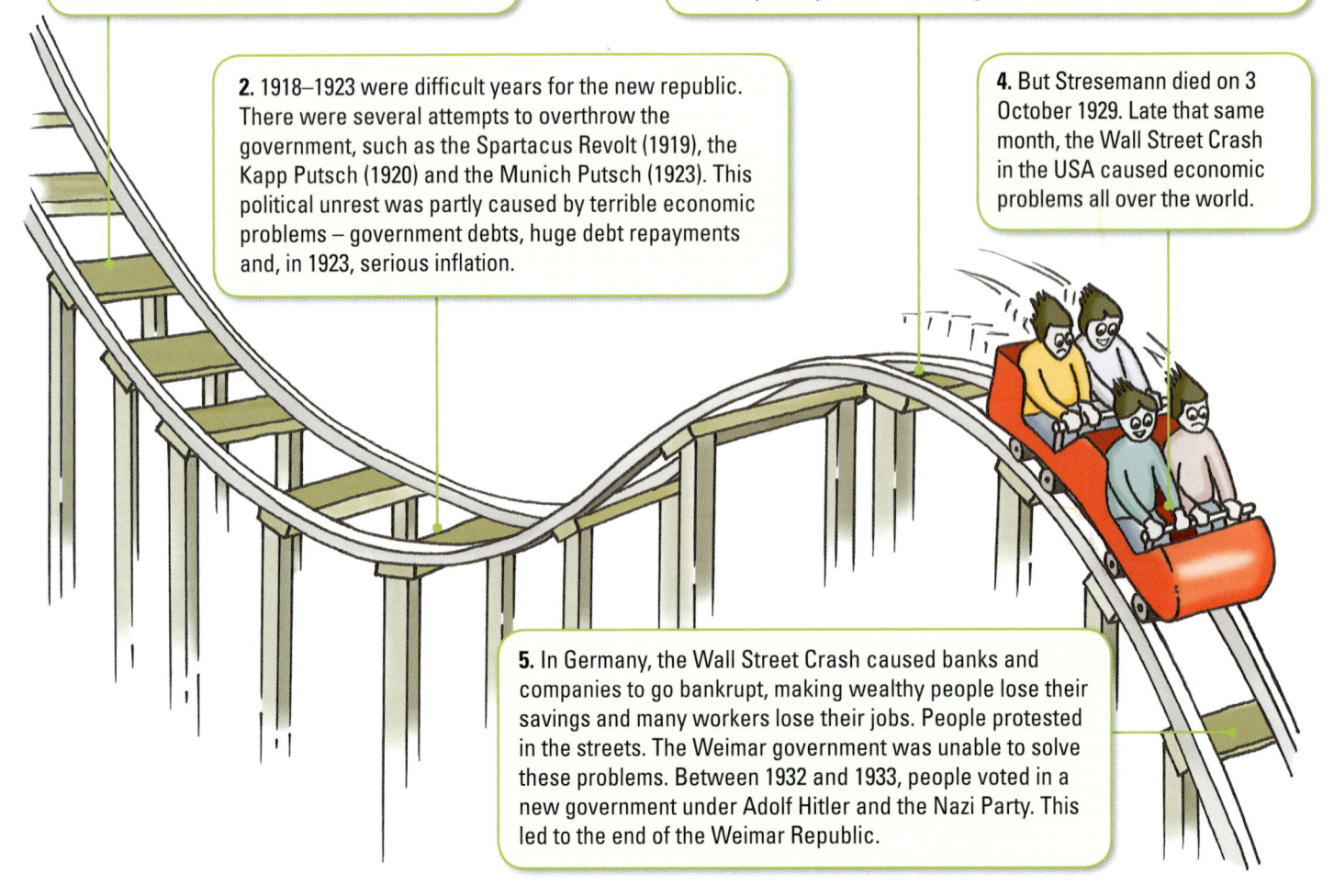

4. But Stresemann died on 3 October 1929. Late that same month, the Wall Street Crash in the USA caused economic problems all over the world.

5. In Germany, the Wall Street Crash caused banks and companies to go bankrupt, making wealthy people lose their savings and many workers lose their jobs. People protested in the streets. The Weimar government was unable to solve these problems. Between 1932 and 1933, people voted in a new government under Adolf Hitler and the Nazi Party. This led to the end of the Weimar Republic.

The Weimar Republic 1918–32

Problems of the new republic

When Kaiser Wilhelm left the country in 1918, Germany's biggest political party, the Social Democratic Party (SPD), formed the first government of the new republic. Friedrich Ebert, an SPD leader, became its first president. Right from the outset, the new republic was weakened by several problems. One was the Treaty of Versailles.

The Treaty of Versailles
On 11 November 1918, Matthias Erzberger, representing the new government, signed the armistice – an agreement to stop fighting. The Allies then drew up the peace treaty. On 28 June 1919, the German delegation signed the Treaty of Versailles.

Source A: A political poster from 1931. It shows a German with hands chained by the shackles of Versailles. Even 12 years after the treaty was signed, political parties still campaigned against it.

Diktat
The treaty was a *diktat* – which meant the Germans were not invited to the negotiations and the treaty was imposed upon them. Because of their military collapse and economic and political problems, they had to accept.

Reparations
In the treaty, Germany had to accept the blame for the First World War. It also said Germany had to pay reparations to the Allies. These were set at £6,600 million. The first repayments were £100 million per year.

Land losses
Germany also had to give up all its colonies and about 13% of its land in Europe – land which contained 50% of its iron and 15% of its coal reserves.

Military losses
Germany's army was cut to 100,000 men. Its navy was limited and it was allowed no air force.

Allies: the countries fighting against Germany in the First World War – originally Britain, France and Russia.

Reparations: money paid by Germany to repay the Allies for their losses in the First World War.

Dolchstoss – the stab in the back
Some Germans said the new republic should have fought on rather than accept the treaty. They said the army had been forced back, not defeated; that the army had been betrayed by politicians in Berlin – 'stabbed in the back'. The leaders of the new republic were blamed for the treaty. They became known as the 'November Criminals'.

Activities
1. Find out more about the Treaty of Versailles. For example, go to www.pearsonhotlinks.co.uk, insert express code 8781P and click on 'Treaty of Versailles'.
2. Decide what Germans hated most about Versailles. Make a case arguing for your choice, perhaps to a partner.
3. What effect did the treaty have on:
   a. the *popularity* of the new republic?
   b. the *strength* of the new republic?

Part A: Carry out a historical enquiry

The Weimar Constitution

Another factor which became a problem for the new republic was its **constitution**. This was decided by the elected National Assembly. Due to unrest in the capital, Berlin, the National Assembly met at Weimar. When the constitution began, the new republic was called the Weimar Republic, even after the government moved back to Berlin.

The new Weimar Constitution

- The constitution was more democratic than government under the Kaiser. German people had more control.

- Proportional representation was used. This meant the number of *Reichstag* seats which political parties were given came from the percentage of votes they gained. This was a true reflection of the wishes of the people.
  But it meant a large number of small, weak political parties in the *Reichstag* – 28 during the 1920s. None of them could ever get a majority on its own.

- There was a system of checks and balances. For example, the *Reichsrat* balanced the power of the *Reichstag*. The president balanced the power of the chancellor. This stopped one person becoming too powerful. But it also prevented quick, strong action in a crisis.

- The *Reichstag* was the most powerful house of the new German parliament; it controlled taxation.
  - Members of the *Reichstag* were elected every four years.
  - All men and women over 20 years of age could vote, using a secret ballot.

- The *Reichsrat* was the other house of the German parliament.
  - A number of members were sent by each local region, according to its size.
  - The *Reichsrat* could delay new laws unless overruled by a two-thirds majority of the *Reichstag*.

- The chancellor was the head of the government. He was normally the head of the largest party. The chancellor chose ministers and ran the country, but to pass laws he needed majority support in the *Reichstag*.

- The president was the head of state – directly elected by the people every seven years. The president took no part in day-to-day government but the president had power:
  - He chose the chancellor.
  - He could dismiss the *Reichstag*, call new elections and assume control of the army.
  - Also, under Article 48, he could suspend the constitution, and pass laws by decree.

Constitution: the rules for governing the country.

Activity

Some aspects of the Weimar Constitution were widely praised as strengths, for example it was very democratic.

But some aspects became weaknesses, for example it produced a large number of small, weak political parties in the *Reichstag*.

Some features could even be considered strengths, in one way, and a weakness, in another.

4. Set out a grid like the one below and describe as many strengths and weaknesses as you can find. Decide which you think is the biggest weakness and justify your answer.

Strengths of the constitution	Weaknesses of the constitution

The Weimar Republic 1918–32

Economic problems, 1918–23

Another problem for the Weimar Republic was a series of economic crises in the period 1918–23.

Bankruptcy

Germany's reserves of gold had all been spent in the war. The Treaty of Versailles took Germany's wealth-earning areas, such as coalfields in Silesia. It also made the German government pay reparations. By 1923 Germany could no longer pay.

Occupation of the Ruhr

In retaliation for non-payment, the French sent troops into the German industrial area of the Ruhr. They confiscated raw materials, manufactured goods and industrial machinery. The Germans bitterly resented this but many Germans also blamed the Weimar government, which seemed powerless to resist.

The occupation of the Ruhr crippled Germany – 80% of German coal, iron and steel were there – worsening Germany's debts, unemployment and shortage of goods.

Inflation

Shortages meant that the price of things went up – this is called inflation. People had to pay more money to get what they needed.

To make matters worse, the government needed money to pay its debts so it just printed more money. In 1923, there were 300 paper mills and 2,000 printing shops just for printing money. The government could now pay reparations but inflation was made much worse. It was a vicious circle: the more prices rose, the more money was printed and this made prices rise again. By 1923, prices were out of control. A loaf of bread cost 1 mark in 1919; by 1922 it cost 200 marks; by November 1923 it cost 200,000 billion marks. This extreme inflation is called hyperinflation.

The results of hyperinflation were complex. A few people benefited. People with debts, for example, suddenly found these much easier to pay back. However, most people suffered and many Germans blamed the Weimar Republic.

- Everyone suffered from shortages. Foreign suppliers refused to accept German money for goods, so imports dried up and shortages of food and other goods got worse – for everyone.
- Everyone found it difficult to buy what they needed – even if their wages went up. People had to carry bundles of money in baskets and even wheelbarrows. Many workers were paid twice a day so they could rush out and buy goods before prices rose again.
- People with savings were hit hardest because their savings became worthless.

Activities

5. Write the following on cards: fall in value of pensions; shortage of goods; bankrupt government; inflation; reparations; fall in value of savings; occupation of the Ruhr; printing more money; Treaty of Versailles.
   - Organise the cards into *causes* and *effects*. Draw lines to link causes and their effects. (Note: some cards may be both a cause of one thing and an effect of another.)
   - What does the diagram say about:
     – the causes of the bankruptcy of the German government?
     – the causes of the social and economic problems of the German people?

Source B: A photograph from 1923 showing children stacking up German banknotes. Hyperinflation had made banknotes almost worthless.

Part A: Carry out a historical enquiry

The political divide, 1918–23

The start of the Weimar Republic was marked by political unrest all over Germany. This unrest came from both right-wing and left-wing groups.

Generally, those on the left wing:
- want to change society rapidly
- aim to treat all people as equals and give political power to workers
- oppose capitalism; they want to abolish private ownership of land and business; they want to put these in the hands of workers
- are internationalist; they stress cooperation of nations.

Socialists are left wing. Communism is an extreme left-wing movement.

Those on the right wing of politics:
- want to keep society stable; stress the importance of the family, law and order, and traditional values
- want a strong government dominated by powerful leaders
- support capitalism – the private ownership of land and business
- are nationalist – placing the interests of the nation over the individual.

Fascism and Nazism are extreme right-wing movements.

In the Weimar Republic, the biggest left-wing party was the KPD – the Communist Party of Germany. It wanted:

- a revolution in Germany like Russia's in 1917
- government by councils of workers or soldiers
- to end private ownership of land and business
- to reduce the power in Germany of the land-owning classes and army leaders.

The right wing in German politics included many small nationalist parties. They gained support from the military leaders, the judiciary and the civil service. They:

- said the Weimar Republic's SPD leaders had betrayed the army in 1918
- hated the communists who had undermined the Kaiser with riots in 1918
- feared the damage communists would do to their property and German traditions
- wanted to reverse Versailles, reinstate the Kaiser and reduce the power of the German people over its leaders.

Source C: A cartoon from 1918 showing Karl Liebknecht, a leading German communist, attacking German property, food supplies, industry, money and families. The cartoon was published by a right-wing group attacking Liebknecht's views.

Activity

6. What does Source C tell you about the beliefs of:
   - German communists?
   - right-wing groups?

The Weimar Republic 1918–32

Political unrest 1918–23

There was almost constant political unrest in Germany from 1918–23, much of it violent. People were bitter and angry about Versailles, unemployment and inflation. Protests took the form of strikes, demonstrations, political assassinations and even attempts to overthrow the government.

The Spartacist Revolt

During the first few months of the new republic, communists in many big German cities tried to overthrow local government and set up workers' and soldiers' councils to run the cities. The biggest uprising took place in the capital, Berlin.

It was led by two communists, Rosa Luxemburg and Karl Liebknecht. They led the Spartacist League – a group named after Spartacus, the head of a slaves' revolt in Ancient Rome. On 6 January 1919, inspired by the Spartacists, 100,000 communists demonstrated in Berlin and took over key buildings, such as newspaper offices.

The army could not put down the revolt alone, so the government turned to the Freikorps. These were about 400,000 demobilised soldiers, who had refused to give back their arms. They were anti-communist and helped the army restore order in the cities. Thousands of communist supporters were arrested or killed, mostly in Berlin. Rosa Luxemburg and Karl Liebknecht were arrested on 15 January; both were murdered by the Freikorps. Leibknecht was shot; Luxemburg was shot in the head and her body dumped in a canal.

The Kapp Putsch

Right-wing groups also tried to overthrow the republic. For example, in March 1920 5,000 right-wing supporters of Dr Wolfgang Kapp mounted a **putsch**. They marched on Berlin to overthrow the Weimar Republic and bring back the Kaiser. For a while, the rebels controlled the city. The government fled to Dresden; they urged people not to cooperate and instead go on strike.

Many workers did strike – they were not right wing and had no desire to see the Kaiser return. Essential services – gas, electricity, water, transport – stopped and the capital ground to a halt. Kapp realised he could not govern and fled. He was caught and put in prison, where he later died.

In 1923, there was another right-wing uprising – the Munich Putsch – led by Adolf Hitler (see page 16). However, after 1923, economic problems subsided and political unrest died down.

> **Follow up your enquiry**
>
> To find out more go to www.pearsonhotlinks.co.uk, insert the express code 8781P and then click on 'the Spartacist Revolt and the Kapp Putsch'. Look at why each group rebelled, what they wanted and how the government had to rely on others to put down the unrest.

> **Did you know?**
>
> The terms 'left' and 'right' to describe political views date back to the new parliament of the French Revolution. Members who wanted to limit change and boost the power of the king sat on the king's right. Those who wanted more change and to give the people more power sat on the king's left.

Putsch: German word for rebellion or revolt.

Source D: The Spartacists were communists. In this KPD poster they are shown fighting to kill German capitalism, militarism and the German landed nobility – the Junker.

Part A: Carry out a historical enquiry

Weimar recovery: the Stresemann era

Activity

7. From late 1923 to 1929, the Weimar Republic enjoyed a period of progress. You could picture the recovery as a wall, like the one below, with economic success and international success as the building blocks of political recovery.

As you read these two pages, construct your own diagram, like the one above. Choose the key details of each of the building blocks of recovery and show them on your diagram. The relevant text has been colour-coded for you.

Solving inflation

In August 1923, during the Ruhr occupation, Gustav Stresemann became the new chancellor. In November, he created the first building block. He achieved a major economic success by solving the problem of inflation.

> First, Stresemann abolished the existing currency and set up a new one, the *Rentenmark*. Then, in 1924, he made this currency safer by putting it under the control of the *Reichsbank*, Germany's national bank, free from government interference.

These changes increased confidence in German currency and helped businesses to recover.

The Dawes Plan, 1924

At the end of 1923, Stresemann lost his post as chancellor. However, he remained in office as foreign secretary and had further success. For example, in 1924 Stresemann agreed the Dawes Plan. This was a big economic success because it helped the government pay its debts.

In 1923, Germany had been unable to pay its reparations repayments. Charles G. Dawes, an American banker, came up with a solution.

> Under the Dawes Plan:
> - annual payments were reduced
> - American banks invested in German industry.

This combined package reassured the Allies that they would get their reparations payments. As a result, the French agreed to leave the Ruhr.

All this improved Germany's economy:

- Industrial output doubled during the period 1923–28, fuelled by US loans.
- Imports and exports increased.
- Employment went up.
- Government income from taxation improved.

Not everyone liked the Dawes Plan. The extreme political parties hated Versailles and were furious that Germany had, again, agreed to pay reparations. Furthermore, the fragile economic recovery depended on American loans. However, most people saw this as an economic success.

The Young Plan, 1929

Stresemann had another economic success with reparations five years later when he agreed the Young Plan. This plan was put forward in August 1929 by an American banker called Owen Young.

> The Young Plan reduced the total reparations debt from £6,600 million to £2,000 million. Moreover, Germany was given 59 years to pay. This was a sensible measure.

- It reduced the government's annual payments. This made it possible to lower taxes. This, in turn, released spending power, which boosted German industry and employment.

Again, not everyone liked the Young Plan:

- The payments were still £50 million per year.
- Furthermore, they now stretched out until 1988.

Several of the extreme political parties were incensed. The increasingly well-known leader of the Nazi Party, Adolf Hitler, said that extending the length of payments was 'passing on the penalty to the unborn'. But the economic successes stabilised prices, boosted jobs and made savings safer. This made people more content and helped political stability.

The Weimar Republic 1918–32

The road to international success

The Locarno Pact, 1925

Stresemann also had successes in international affairs.

In December 1925 the Locarno Pact was signed. This was a treaty between Germany, Britain, France, Italy and Belgium.

Germany agreed to keep its new 1919 border with France and Belgium.

In return:
- Allied troops left the Rhineland
- France promised peace with Germany.

Wartime defeat

Some political parties resented the fact that the hated Versailles borders had been confirmed.

But many Germans saw the Locarno Pact as a success; Germany was treated as an equal, not dictated to.

The League of Nations

At the end of the First World War, the Allies had founded the League of Nations. This was a new international body in which powerful countries discussed ways of solving the world's problems. But Germany had been excluded from membership. In September 1926, Stresemann persuaded the other great powers to accept Germany as a member.

Germany was given a place on the Council of the League of Nations – which took the League's biggest decisions.

Not all political parties were pleased. To some, the League was a symbol of the hated Treaty of Versailles.

However, Stresemann's view was different. He saw it as another step towards German equality with other nations.

Kellogg–Briand Pact

In August 1928, Germany became one of 65 countries to sign the Kellogg–Briand Pact, an international agreement in which states promised not to use war to achieve their foreign-policy aims.

International respect

It was not Stresemann's idea, but it was another sign that he had persuaded others to see Germany as a respectable member of the international community.

Stresemann and his French counterpart, Briand, were awarded the Nobel Peace Prize for improving relations between the two countries.

It was also one more thing to make moderate Germans feel that the Weimar Republic was becoming a success and it helped political stability.

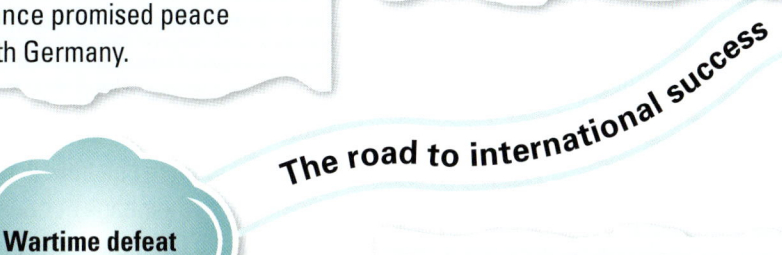

Political stability

Under the influence of Stresemann, economic and international successes had made the German public much happier with the Weimar Republic. As a result, by 1929, Germany was much more settled and stable, both politically and socially.

However, on 3 October 1929, Stresemann died. Then later that month, the world was hit by the Wall Street Crash (see page 12). Stability in Germany ended.

Follow up your enquiry

By 1929, Germany was enjoying a more settled period of social and political stability. Go to www.pearsonhotlinks.co.uk, insert express code 8781P and click on 'Towards prosperity and hope' to watch a video and decide whether it supports this statement.

Activity

8. Look back over all the things the Weimar Republic did in the period 1918–29. Draw up a balance sheet of its successes and failures by the end of September 1929. Overall, how had it done? Discuss your answer with a partner to see if you agree.

Part A: Carry out a historical enquiry

Economic crisis, 1929–32: the Great Depression

1. The Wall Street Crash

In October 1929, share prices began to fall on the Wall Street stock exchange in New York.

Falling shares meant people's investments fell in value.

Worried about losing money, people were desperate to sell shares before they fell further. On 'Black Thursday', 24 October 1929, 13 million shares were sold.

But this panic selling sent prices even lower. Shares worth $20,000 in the morning were worth only $1,000 by the end of the day's trading.

Within a week, investors lost $4,000 million. This is called the Wall Street Crash.

The Wall Street Crash sent economic shockwaves across the world.

2. Economic crisis in the USA caused a **Great Depression** – a severe downturn in the economy – all over the world. It caused problems for Germany.

3. Banks all over the world had invested heavily in shares and so they suffered huge losses. German banks lost so much money that people feared the banks wouldn't be able to pay out the money in their bank accounts. People rushed to German banks to get their money back – causing some banks to run out of cash.

4. And there was a further problem for the German economy. Banks all over the world urgently needed the return of money they had lent to German businesses. But German companies were dependent upon these loans. They either had to cut their staff or close. German industrial output fell and unemployment rose.

5. All kinds of German businesses suffered – whether they normally sold their goods in Germany or abroad. The worldwide depression was a disaster for German export industries. But high unemployment meant that demand for goods fell inside Germany too. Unemployment rose further.

Years	Fall in industrial production (per cent)
1929–30	10%
1929–31	30%
1929–32	40%

As the depression deepened, German industrial production fell and fell.

Date	Unemployment
September 1929	1.3 million
September 1931	4.3 million
September 1932	5.1 million
January 1933	6.0 million

As industry suffered, unemployment increased.

ResultsPlus Watch out

Make sure that you are clear that the Wall Street Crash happened in the United States – not in Germany. But problems in the USA affected Germany badly because the German economy depdended on US loans.

Social and political effects

The economic collapse caused suffering. The middle classes lost savings, their companies or their homes. Workers became unemployed.

People demanded political action, but the Weimar Government failed them. From 1930 to 1932, the chancellor was Heinrich Brüning. He proposed:

- raising taxes to pay the cost of unemployment benefit
- reducing unemployment benefit to make the payments more affordable.

This pleased no one. Right-wing parties, the middle classes and the wealthy opposed higher taxes. Left-wing parties and the working classes opposed lower benefits.

The coalition of parties which the government depended upon collapsed in 1930. Brüning could govern only with the help of presidential decree. There had only been five presidential decrees in 1930. As the crisis deepened, Brüning's government had to rely on 44 decrees in 1931 and 66 in 1932.

But even this was no use – the causes of suffering were beyond government control and the crisis continued. Useless decrees just undermined confidence in the Weimar Republic still further.

The unemployed roamed the streets; some joined the private armies of political parties. Violent clashes became common. Brüning had lost control of the *Reichstag*, the economy and the streets. He resigned in 1932, leaving a dangerous power vacuum for a new leader to step into.

Source E: This is a quotation from an eyewitness, Kurt Lüdecke, in 1930.

> Four private armies, with knives, revolvers and knuckle-dusters rampaged through towns – the SA of the Nazis, the Red Front of the KDP, the Sozi of the SPD and the Stahlhelm. The Reichswehr [the army] were nowhere.

Source F: A Nazi cartoon showing Brüning's government propped up only by a rickety combination of weak bans (*Verbote*), taxes (*Steuern*), regulations (*Ordnung*) and decrees issued under Article 48.

Your conclusion so far

In this section of the book, we have seen that:

- The German Kaiser abdicated in 1918 and was replaced by the Weimar Republic.
- The new republic had to accept the humiliation of the Treaty of Versailles in 1919.
- Economic and political problems plagued the early years of the Weimar Republic, 1918–23.
- The work of Gustav Stresemann helped the Weimar Republic to recover in the years 1924–29.
- The death of Stresemann and a world economic crisis threw the Weimar Republic into turmoil in 1929.

What was the impact of the Great Depression on Germany in the years 1929–32?

- Make a list of the effects and write each one on a card.
- Organise the cards into economic, social and political effects.
- Some effects are linked, for example unemployment was linked to political unrest. What other links can you find?

Part A: Carry out a historical enquiry

A2 Hitler and the growth of the Nazi Party 1918–33

Learning outcomes
By the end of this topic, you should be able to:
- describe the main events of the Nazi Party's growth in the years up to 1933
- understand the beliefs of the Nazi Party
- explain the reasons for its success.

Hitler and the Nazi Party, 1919–23

Hitler's early life

Adolf Hitler was born in Braunau, in Austria, on 20 April 1889. He was, therefore, an Austrian, not a German. Hitler tried and failed to earn a living as an artist in Vienna, the capital of Austria. There was a strong anti-Jewish movement in Vienna at that time. Hitler began to blame the Jews for his own failure. He said Jews dominated industry and the arts and ruined chances for people like him.

Looking for success elsewhere, Hitler moved to Munich, in Germany. So, in 1914, when the First World War broke out, he joined the German Army. Hitler was a good soldier. He became a corporal and was awarded the Iron Cross for bravery. So the defeat of Germany was a blow to Hitler. He believed that the German Army had never been defeated. He insisted that it was 'betrayed' by the 'traitors' who agreed to peace. He said Germany was 'stabbed in the back' by socialists and Jews.

Activity

1. From the text above, work out two beliefs which Hitler developed by 1918 which were based on the experiences of his early life.

Did you know?
Hitler's father was born Alois Schicklgruber. He changed his name to Hitler before Adolf was born. Perhaps this was good for Hitler. 'Heil Schicklgruber' hasn't the same ring to it!

The DAP

After the war, Hitler was given an army assignment checking up on political groups. One of these was the German Workers' Party (DAP), a group founded in January 1919 by Anton Drexler.

The DAP was a tiny movement at this point. Hitler attended two meetings in September 1919; there were only 23 people present at the first meeting and 40 at the second. At Hitler's third meeting, the treasurer announced its entire funds – 7 marks and 50 pfennig (enough to buy 15lbs of sugar at the time). But Hitler was attracted by the party's main views. It said:

- the communists and socialists were to blame for bringing down the Kaiser
- the Weimar politicians had let Germany down by accepting the Treaty of Versailles
- democratic states are weak states
- the Jews were to blame for undermining the German economy.

During the autumn of 1919, Hitler joined the DAP.

The 25-point Programme

By 1920, Hitler was working as Drexler's right-hand man. In February 1920, they revealed the new 25-point Programme of the DAP. It said:

- the Treaty of Versailles should be scrapped
- Germany's borders should be expanded to give its people *Lebensraum* – more land to live in
- Jews should be refused German citizenship.

The programme also made clear that the DAP was willing to use force to achieve all this.

From 1920, Hitler's role in the DAP grew. Then he became party leader and established absolute personal control of the party. The diagram on the opposite page shows how he did this.

Hitler and the growth of the Nazi Party 1918–33

Public speaking and membership

Hitler's passionate speeches started to draw larger numbers to meetings. His views attracted many people who were dissatisfied with the Weimar Republic, including people from the army, the police and small businesses. As a result membership grew to about 3,000 by late 1920.

Source A: A quotation from Carl Suckmayer, who heard Hitler speak in Munich in 1923. He said he was close enough to see spit flying from under his moustache.

> This man…knew how to fire up the people – not with arguments, impossible in hate speeches – but with the fanaticism of his whole manner, screaming and yelling, and above all by deafening repetition, and a certain contagious rhythm…it has a fearfully exciting primitive and barbaric effect.

Party organisation

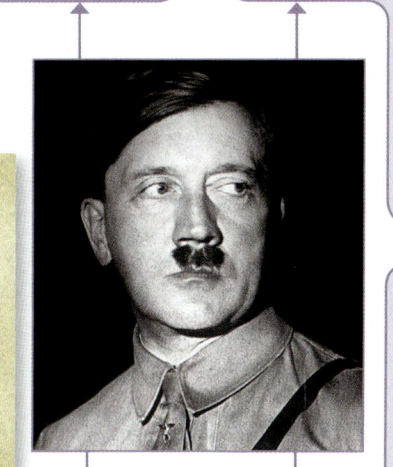

During 1920, at Hitler's suggestion, the DAP changed its name to the National Socialist German Workers' Party (NSDAP, or Nazi Party for short). He made it his own party, with the swastika as its emblem and the raised arm salute. Increased membership boosted funds and the party was able to buy a newspaper – the *Völkischer Beobachter* – to spread Hitler's views.

Source B: An SPD poster from 1922 showing an SA trooper with brown uniform and swastika. It says 'Your enemy is on the right. Choose the Social Democrats!' Even this early, the SPD thought that the NSDAP was a threat.

Party leadership

In mid-1921, Hitler pushed Drexler aside and became the party Führer, or leader. He kept control by gathering personal supporters around him:

- Rudolf Hess, a wealthy academic who became Hitler's deputy
- Julius Streicher, founder of another Nazi paper, *Der Stürmer*.

Hitler also cultivated powerful friends, such as General Ludendorff, leader of the German Army during the First World War.

The SA – *Sturmabteilung*

In 1921, Hitler created the *Sturmabteilung* (SA), or storm troopers. They were the party's private army, recruited from demobbed soldiers, the unemployed and students. These 'Brownshirts' provided security at meetings and bodyguards for Nazi leaders; they also broke up meetings of opposition groups. Hitler put Ernst Röhm in charge of the SA.

Many of the SA were thugs and difficult to control, so in 1923 Hitler selected trusted members of the SA and formed his own personal bodyguard, the *Stosstrupp* or 'Shock troop'.

Source C: An extract from *Adolf Hitler* by John Toland, 1976, describing a DAP meeting in 1920.

> Hitler's army supporters, tough as leather and hard as Krupp steel, eagerly went into battle armed with rubber truncheons and riding whips. Troublemakers were hustled away, order was restored and Hitler resumed speaking.

Activity

2. - Make a list of the beliefs of the early Nazi Party which contributed to its success.
   - Make a list of other factors which helped to make the early Nazi Party a success.
   - Compare your lists with a partner's.

Part A: Carry out a historical enquiry

The Munich Putsch, 1923

In November 1923, Hitler launched the Munich Putsch – an uprising against the German government. Remember the Spartacist Revolt and the Kapp Putsch. Revolts against the Weimar Republic were not uncommon at this time.

Causes

Hitler had three reasons for launching a rebellion against the German government at this precise time.

First, it was 1923. Hyperinflation was making the lives of all Germans miserable. People were also angry about the French occupation of the Ruhr. The Weimar government seemed to have done nothing about this. It seemed weak. Hitler wanted to exploit this discontent. Membership of the NSDAP had grown to about 55,000 by 1923 but most of these were people from around Munich, the capital of Bavaria, in the south of Germany. This was Hitler's chance to make an impact nationally.

Second, Hitler sensed that the new government of Gustav Stresemann would soon get on top of Germany's economic and international problems. He needed to act before unrest died down.

Third, Stresemann's government was starting to crack down on extremist groups. The army had recently put down a left-wing revolt in Saxony. Hitler could see a crackdown on right-wing groups coming next.

Events

So Hitler decided to act. On the evening of 8 November 1923, there was a meeting of 3,000 officials of the Bavarian government in a beer hall, called the Bürgerbräukeller, in Munich. The three main speakers were:

- Kahr, the leader of the Bavarian government
- Seisser, the head of the Bavarian police
- Lossow, the head of the army in Bavaria.

Hitler burst into the meeting with 600 SA storm troopers, waving a gun. He fired a shot into the ceiling and said that he was taking over the government of Bavaria. He claimed that, after taking control in Munich, he would then march against the German government. He was supported by the famous German general, Erich Ludendorff.

Kahr, Seisser and Lossow were taken off into a side room. Confronted with Hitler, his troops and their weapons, they agreed to support the uprising. At this point, the revolt seemed to be going well. But next morning, Hitler heard that Kahr, Seisser and Lossow had changed their minds and opposed him. This was a blow. The SA had only 2,000 rifles, far fewer than the local police and army forces, but Hitler pressed on.

Hitler sent 3,000 supporters to key buildings around the town, each group supported by the SA. Hitler, his key supporters and his Stosstrupp marched on the town centre to declare him the president of Germany. But they were met by state police, who opened fire.

Source D: A photograph of Hitler's Shock Troop on the morning of the Munich Putsch.

Hitler and the growth of the Nazi Party 1918–33

A bodyguard, Graf, threw himself in front of Hitler and was hit by several bullets. Goering fell, shot in the thigh. Hitler was dragged to the ground by his bodyguards with such force that his left arm was dislocated. In all, 14 of Hitler's supporters and four police were killed.

Ludendorff was arrested. Other rebels fled; one group entered a nearby ladies' academy and hid under the beds. Hitler fled the scene in a car. He hid at the house of a friend, ten miles south of Munich, but was later found and arrested.

Results

Hitler and several other leaders were put on trial. He was found guilty – so some of the results were bad for the Nazis. However, the results of the Munich Putsch were by no means all bad for Hitler.

Did you know?

Hitler spent two days hiding in the attic at his friend's house after the failure of the Munich Putsch. The family gardener informed police and Hitler was arrested after he was found hiding in a wardrobe.

Activity

3. Two reasons why the Munich Putsch did not succeed are:
- losing the support of Kahr, Seisser and Lossow
- too few armed supporters.

    Was one of these reasons more important than the other?

    Is there any way they are connected?

Was the Munich Putsch a failure?

- Hitler was convicted of treason – betraying his country – and sentenced to five years in gaol at Landsberg Castle.
  The NSDAP was banned.
  In the short term, the Munich Putsch was therefore a defeat and a humiliation for Hitler

- Hitler was released after only nine months.

- Hitler used his trial to get national publicity for his views and sympathy for his party.

- The ban on the NSDAP was weakly enforced and then lifted in 1925. In fact, as a result of the publicity, the NSDAP won its first seats in the Reichstag – 32 seats in the May 1924 election.

- Hitler used his time in gaol to write his autobiography – *Mein Kampf* (My struggle). It contained his political ideas and became the guiding light of the Nazi Party.

- Finally, Hitler realised he needed a new approach to gain power in Germany (see Source E).

- However the judge was quite lenient – five years was the minimum sentence allowed for treason. Ludendorff, incredibly, was even found not guilty.

Activity

4. Look at the events and the results of the Munich Putsch.
   - List three reasons why it could be considered a failure.
   - List three reasons why it could be considered a success.

   Overall, do you think it was a success or a failure?

Source E: An extract from a letter written by Hitler from gaol. The strategy he describes did later get him into power.

> Instead of…an armed coup, we shall have to hold our noses and enter the Reichstag…If out-voting them takes longer than out-shooting them, at least the result will be guaranteed…Sooner or later we shall have a majority and, after that – Germany!

17

Part A: Carry out a historical enquiry

The rebirth of Nazism, 1924

Hitler left prison in 1924 with a clearer vision for his Nazi Party. There are several places where we can see what Hitler's Nazi Party stood for:

- *Mein Kampf*, Hitler's blueprint for the party
- Hitler's *Second Book* or 'Secret Book', which he wrote in 1928, though it was not published until 1959, well after he died
- Hitler's speeches, publications and actions, including the Nazi Party **manifesto** of 1933 (see Sources F and G).

They make the beliefs of National Socialism, or Nazism, very clear.

Nationalism

This meant that the Nazi Party wanted to:

- put the needs of the nation above everything and revive German power
- break the restrictions on Germany in the Treaty of Versailles
- make Germany self-sufficient and not dependent on imports (known as 'autarky')
- expand Germany's borders
- purify the German 'race'.

Socialism

Like the communists, Hitler wanted to control big businesses. But communists wanted to put all private land and businesses into the hands of the workers. Hitler did not support this form of socialism. To him, socialism meant government running the economy in the national interest so that:

- businesses would not make unfair profits
- both agriculture and industry would flourish
- workers would be treated fairly.

Totalitarianism

This was the belief that the Nazi Party should *totally* control every aspect of life.

Hitler despised democracy. He said it was weak. He believed in the *Führerprinzip* (leadership principle); this meant total loyalty to the leader. This way, he said, the leader could organise every aspect of society for the benefit of the German people.

Manifesto: a list of political party promises to voters.

Source F: An extract from the 1933 Nazi Party manifesto.

> Standing above…classes, [the National Government] will bring back to our people… political unity…The National Government will [save]…the German farmer so that the nation's food supply…shall be secured [and save] the German worker by a massive…attack on unemployment.

Activity

5. Use these two pages (18–19) to identify ten policies the Nazi Party believed in. Write each on a card.

   Give each policy, one at a time, to a partner and see if they can put each one under one (or more) of the following headings:
   - Nationalism
   - Socialism
   - Totalitarianism
   - Traditional German values
   - Struggle
   - Racial purity.

ResultsPlus
Watch out

Students sometimes get confused about the 'socialist' in the Nazi Party title – the National Socialist German Workers' Party. The Nazi Party was not a left-wing socialist party like the SPD. Hitler did not want to put all land and business into the hands of workers, as the socialists did. But it suited his purpose to put 'socialist' in the title of the party. It made the Nazis seem like a party for the working classes.

Traditional German values

Hitler said that moral and cultural values had been weakened in the Weimar Republic. He said the Nazis would work for the return of:

- strong family values, with clear male and female roles
- Christian morality
- old-style German culture, with traditional art, music and theatre.

Source G: An extract from the 1933 Nazi Party manifesto.

> We shall take Christianity as the basis for our morality and the family as the nucleus of our nation and state.

Struggle

Hitler believed that life was a contest in which people constantly struggled against each other. He even called his blueprint for the Nazi Party *Mein Kampf* – My struggle.

He said that this constant struggle made people and countries healthier and fitter. Nazis believed that Germany should struggle:

- outside her borders, against other countries, for land – to get *Lebensraum* (living space), so that all German people could live together, united
- inside her borders, against non-German people, so that they could strengthen the true German race.

This made the Nazi Party aggressive towards other countries and other groups within Germany.

Follow up your enquiry

Find out more about *Mein Kampf*. Use other text books and the internet. For example, go to www.pearsonhotlinks.co.uk, insert the express code 8781P and then click on '*Mein Kampf*'. Note down any other ideas in *Mein Kampf* which you have not been told about on these pages.

Racial purity

Hitler and the Nazis said that people were divided into superior and inferior races.

According to Hitler, the Aryans were the superior race. These were the Germanic people of northern Europe, who, he said, had produced all that was good in human culture.

He believed that other races, from places like Eastern Europe (for example, the Slavs), and from Asia and Africa, were inferior races.

The lowest form of life, he said, were the Jews, whom he described as parasites who fed off the countries they lived in.

Source H: A Nazi poster from 1924 showing the combination of dominant working man and the woman as the mother figure – both of them serving the national flag.

Part A: Carry out a historical enquiry

Activity

6. Be the author! This page has a main heading but it has no subheadings. Put yourself in the place of the author. As you read this page, choose subheadings that would point out to the reader the key features of Nazi Party organisation 1924–29. For example, you could start with 'Relaunch'. Under each of your subheadings, list the key points of the key feature you have identified.

Nazi Party organisation in the lean years, 1924–29

Hitler relaunched the Nazi Party on 27 February 1925 – ironically at the Bürgerbräukeller, scene of the Munich Putsch. He had lost none of his personal appeal: 4,000 people heard him speak; a further thousand had to be turned away.

Hitler appointed two efficient organisers to run Nazi headquarters: Philipp Bouhler as secretary and Franz Schwarz as treasurer. He also divided the party into regions; he appointed a network of *Gauleiters*, answerable only to him, who ran the NSDAP in each *Gau*, or region.

To fund all this, Hitler improved party finances. He befriended Germany's most wealthy businessmen. They shared his hatred of communism and hoped Hitler would limit the power of trade unions. By the early 1930s, the Nazis were receiving donations from giants of German industry, such as Thyssen, Krupp and Bosch.

This extra income also helped Hitler to expand the SA. It had 400,000 members by 1930. But the Munich Putsch had taught Hitler the importance of a totally loyal bodyguard – and Hitler didn't trust the SA.

Many storm troopers were violent thugs and difficult to control, and while Hitler was in prison the SA had developed a dangerous loyalty to Ernst Röhm, its commander. So, in 1925, Hitler set up a new party security group. He called them the *Schutzstaffel* (Protection squad), or SS.

At first, the SS was run by Hitler's personal chauffeur and bodyguard, Julius Schreck, and soon after by Heinrich Himmler, one of his most loyal supporters. The SS became famous – and feared – for their menacing black uniforms (introduced in 1932).

Hitler also worked with Dr Joseph Goebbels to improve Nazi party **propaganda**. Hitler and Goebbels had a simple message, but they created many ways to get it across.

They created scapegoats whom they blamed for Germany's problems: the Jews, the communists and the moderate leaders of the Weimar Republic – especially the Social Democrats, who had signed the Armistice and Treaty of Versailles.

They promoted Hitler as the voice of the Nazi Party. By the 1930s, his speeches were reported in 120 daily or weekly Nazi newspapers, read by hundreds of thousands of Germans across the whole country.

They used the most up-to-date technology, including radio, films and gramophone records, to keep Hitler in the public eye. Hitler used aeroplanes to fly from venue to venue, so that he could speak in up to five cities a day.

They created a clear image for the party – an image of strength. The image was set by:

- Hitler's passion
- the spectacle of mass Nazi rallies
- the impressive power of the SA and the SS.

Source I: An extract from *Mein Kampf*, written by Hitler.

> Propaganda must confine itself to very few points and repeat them endlessly. Here, persistence is the first and foremost condition of success.

Propaganda: information or ideas used to influence people's attitudes and beliefs.

Why 'lean years'?

By 1929, the Nazi Party was well organised. It had 100,000 members and Hitler was a national figure. But from 1923, inflation had eased, employment had increased and people were better off.

Under Stresemann, Germany was becoming important again on the world stage. In 1925, Hindenburg, the 78-year-old German Army ex-field marshal, had become president; his reputation made more people support the Weimar Republic.

As a result, these were lean years for the Nazis. Voters supported moderate parties, such as the SPD, and all the extreme parties lost ground. In the general elections of May 1928, the Nazis:

- won only 12 seats
- were only the ninth biggest *Reichstag* party
- polled only 810,000 votes – just 2.6% of the national vote.

Source J: An extract from a confidential report on the Nazis by the Interior Ministry, July 1927.

> A numerically insignificant…splinter group incapable of exerting any noticeable influence on the great mass of the people and the course of political events.

Activity

7. Pages 14–21 of this book tell you about Hitler and the Nazi Party up to 1929.

   a. Look back at these pages and decide how well Hitler and the Nazi Party have done so far.

   b. Make a table, like the one below, to record your views.

Nazi Party successes and progress by 1929	Nazi Party failures and shortcomings by 1929

   c. Finally, compare your views with those of others in your group.

Follow up your enquiry

Look more widely for ideas for your table about Nazi Party progress. Use other books and the internet. For example, go to www.pearsonhotlinks.co.uk, insert the express code 8781P and then click on 'Nazi Party'. Use your further research to add to your table.

Source K: A photograph of the *Schutzstaffel*, or SS. Note the number of men, the quality of their uniforms – all identical – and their discipline; these all suggest a well-financed, well-organised movement.

Part A: Carry out a historical enquiry

Nazi support grows, 1929–32

In October 1929, share prices crashed on Wall Street, the US stock exchange (see pages 12–13). American banks recalled loans to German industries and banks, causing many to close. Rising unemployment brought suffering to working people and the middle classes (see pages 12–13). Unrest increased as people demonstrated in the streets.

Heinrich Brüning, who became chancellor in 1930, could not get a majority in the *Reichstag* and had to govern by presidential decree. He tried raising taxes to pay benefits to the poor. He tried banning demonstrations to calm unrest. Both failed. Voters turned to extreme right-wing and left-wing parties to solve their problems.

General elections 1928–32: seats in the Reichstag and votes

	May 1928	Sept 1930	July 1932
Nazi seats	12	107	230
Communist seats	54	77	89
Nazi votes	1 million	6 million	14 million

But we need to understand why German voters supported the Nazis rather than other parties. Some reasons appealed to many voters across all classes. For example, they had a strong leader and a private army, the SA.

The strength of the SA

By 1930, the SA had 400,000 storm troopers. The SA was used in rallies to make the Nazi Party seem strong, organised, disciplined and reliable. They gave people hope for the future. They were also used to disrupt opposition parties. The elections of 1930 and 1932 were violent. Armed, uniformed men tore down posters for the opposition, intimidated their candidates, broke into their offices and disrupted their rallies. Voters were also intimidated outside polling stations.

Activity

8. Create a table like the one below:

Who supported the Nazis?	Why they supported the Nazis

- As you read these two pages, fill in the columns in your table.
- When you have finished, compare your table with someone sitting near you.

Hitler's appeal

Hitler was one of the reasons people turned to the Nazis. He was the party's figurehead. He appeared everywhere. He used aeroplanes in a whirlwind campaign for the 1930 and 1932 elections. Germans saw him as man who could:

- unite the country under a strong leader
- restore order from social unrest
- scrap the Treaty of Versailles
- persuade other nations to treat Germany fairly.

Hitler's powerful speeches were an important part of his appeal.

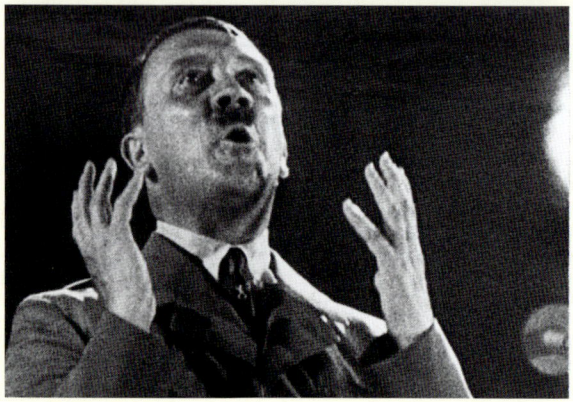

Hitler and the growth of the Nazi Party 1918–33

The Nazis' appeal to specific groups

Working-class support

Many working-class people were attracted by Nazi support for traditional German values and a strong Germany.

The Nazis promised workers 'Work and Bread' on posters. As the poorest class, this promise was powerful.

The Nazis also used posters which gave the impression that lots of working people already supported the Nazis. And, of course, they called themselves the National Socialist German *Workers* Party.

The working class were the biggest group of voters. But the Nazis never dominated the working-class vote. When times were hard, many workers supported the communists, so Nazi working-class support was important; but it wasn't enough.

Middle-class support

The middle class contained professional people, like teachers and lawyers, business people and small farmers. They often owned land or businesses and had savings. Between 1929 and 1932, they deserted more moderate parties, like the Social Democrats, and supported the Nazis. There were several reasons for this.

The Great Depression hurt the middle classes. Many lost their companies, their savings or their pensions. They saw Hitler as a strong leader who could help the country recover.

They were also afraid of the growing Communist Party after 1929. The communists wanted to abolish private ownership of land and businesses. The middle classes saw the Nazis as a strong party which could protect them from the communists.

There was also a view that there had been a moral decline under the Weimar Republic, including more drinking and sexual openness. The Nazis represented a return to traditional German values. This went down well with the middle classes.

Farmers

The Nazis targeted farmers in particular.

The Nazi policy of confiscating all private land (in the 25-point programme of 1920) was changed in 1928. The new policy said that private land would only be confiscated if owned by Jews.

This way, Hitler could promise to protect the farmers from the Communist Party, which would have confiscated their land.

How the Nazis appealed to specific groups of voters

Big business

The wealthy business classes usually supported the National Party. But this party, like other moderate parties, got smaller after 1929 – its *Reichstag* seats halved. Industrialists saw Hitler as protection from the rise of the communists.

The support of wealthy business leaders boosted Nazi finances and gave them the support of powerful newspaper owners, like Alfred Hugenberg.

Young people and women

The young were attracted by Hitler's passionate speeches, his ambitions for the future and the atmosphere of Nazi rallies.

At first, women did not support the Nazis, whose policies towards women restricted them. But, Nazi propaganda made special appeals to women. It said that voting for the NSDAP was best for their country and best for their families.

Activity

9. With a partner, debate the following statement:
   The Germans were not really enthusiastic about the Nazis. They were just desperate for someone to solve their problems.
   One of you should argue for enthusiasm. The other should argue for desperation.
   Who won the debate?

ResultsPlus
Top Tip

Don't forget that the suffering caused by the Great Depression was an important reason for the growth in support for the Nazis.

Part A: Carry out a historical enquiry

The Nazis win power, 1932–33

In March 1932, Hitler stood as a candidate in the presidential elections. His main rivals were Hindenburg, president since 1925, and Ernst Thälmann, leader of the Communist Party.

We have seen that this was a time of economic depression, unemployment and lost savings. As in the general elections, many people showed their desperation by voting for extreme candidates. The votes (in millions) were as follows.

Hindenburg	Thälmann	Hitler
18m votes	5m votes	11m votes

Because no candidate had achieved 50 per cent of the vote, the election was repeated in April.

Hindenburg	Thälmann	Hitler
19m votes	4m votes	13m votes

Hindenburg was re-elected. But Hitler was now a significant figure with a large national following.

The fall of Chancellor Brüning

In April 1932, the moderate socialist chancellor, Brüning, used a presidential decree to ban the SA and SS. He wanted to calm unrest and control the Nazis. But right-wing parties were angered. An ambitious general, Kurt von Schleicher, decided to remove Brüning. He organised a coalition of right-wing groups, consisting of landowners, industrialists and army officers. Then he persuaded Hindenburg that they had a majority in the *Reichstag*, and Brüning was sacked.

Papen becomes chancellor

Schleicher controlled the new government from behind the scenes. He chose a wealthy politician, ex-General Franz von Papen, as the figurehead for this new coalition. In May 1932, Hindenburg made Papen chancellor.

Schleicher offered the NSDAP a place in the coalition. He thought he could control the Nazis, seeing them as 'merely children who had to be led by the hand'. Hitler agreed to the offer. From May 1932, therefore, Hitler and the Nazi Party were, for the first time, part of the government of Germany.

Activity

10. Use the list of events below to make a flight of steps to show Hitler's rise to power. Each of the events should be a step. A big step towards power should be tall; a smaller step towards power should be less tall.

- the presidential elections in 1932
- Papen made chancellor May 1932
- the *Reichstag* elections July 1932
- the *Reichstag* elections November 1932
- Schleicher made chancellor December 1932
- Hitler made chancellor January 1933.

Write a paragraph explaining your steps diagram.

But Papen's coalition was in trouble from the start. When the general elections of July 1932 were held, the NSDAP won 230 seats in the *Reichstag*. It was now the largest party. This enabled Hitler to demand that Hindenburg should sack Papen and appoint him chancellor.

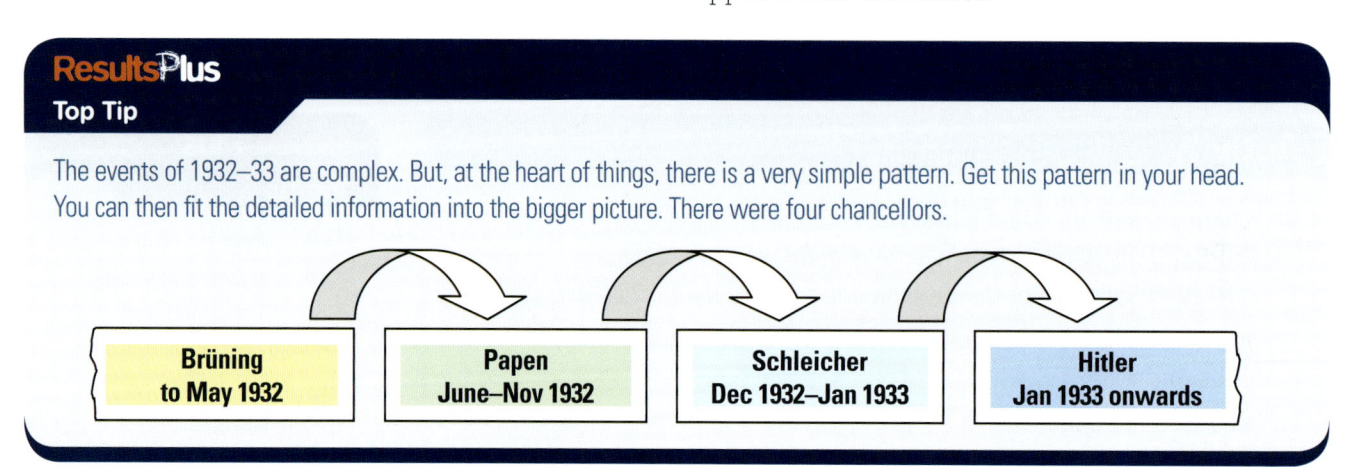

ResultsPlus
Top Tip

The events of 1932–33 are complex. But, at the heart of things, there is a very simple pattern. Get this pattern in your head. You can then fit the detailed information into the bigger picture. There were four chancellors.

Brüning to May 1932 → Papen June–Nov 1932 → Schleicher Dec 1932–Jan 1933 → Hitler Jan 1933 onwards

Hindenburg, a field marshal of German forces during the First World War, detested Hitler – in his eyes he was a vulgar, jumped-up corporal. He refused. Instead, Papen hung on to office and called a new election for November 1932. He was gambling that the Nazi support would fall.

Nazi seats in the *Reichstag* did fall to 196, but they were still the largest party. Papen lost his gamble. Without Hitler's support, he no longer had a majority in the *Reichstag*; he resigned.

Schleicher becomes chancellor

Hindenburg still refused to make Hitler chancellor. On 2 December, he appointed Schleicher.

Schleicher was confident that support for the Nazis was fading. He told a visiting Austrian minister that 'Herr Hitler is no longer a problem; his movement is a thing of the past'. But Schleicher was unable to govern; he had no majority in the *Reichstag*. In desperation, he asked Hindenburg to suspend the constitution and make Schleicher head of a military **dictatorship**. Hindenburg refused, but news of Schleicher's plan leaked out. He lost any remaining support in the *Reichstag*. His time was up.

Hitler becomes chancellor

Papen said he had the solution. He told Hindenburg and right-wing parties in the *Reichstag* that they should make Hitler the chancellor. He also said they should make him, Papen, the vice-chancellor, so they could make all the decisions themselves and use Hitler as a figurehead. He said he had Hitler 'in his pocket'.

So, reluctantly, Hindenburg agreed that there was no alternative. 'It is my unpleasant duty then to appoint this fellow Hitler as chancellor', he grumbled. On 30 January 1933, Adolf Hitler was legally and democratically appointed chancellor of Germany.

Dictatorship: a state governed by one person who has total control.

Source L: This 1933 British cartoon shows Hindenburg and Papen lifting Hitler to power, while cursing him under their breath.

Your conclusion so far

In this section of the book, we have seen how:

- the Nazi Party was formed (1920–22)
- Hitler failed to win power in the Munich Putsch
- Hitler rebuilt the Nazi Party (1924–29)
- economic depression helped the Nazis come to power (1929–33).

Think about these factors in Nazi Party success:

- German bitterness about Versailles
- German economic problems
- weaknesses in the Weimar Constitution
- Hitler's personal appeal.

Was any one of these the key reason for Nazi success in the years 1920–33? Or was it a combination of all or some of them?

Part A: Carry out a historical enquiry

A3 The Nazi dictatorship 1933–39

Learning outcomes
By the end of this topic, you should be able to:
- understand the ways in which Hitler created a Nazi dictatorship
- understand the ways in which Hitler maintained this dictatorship.

Activity
1. As you read pages 26–29, make a table showing the things Hitler did to take total power of Germany.

   Organise your table in two columns, dividing what Hitler did into two types of action – legal and illegal.

   You will use this table in the activity on page 29.

The removal of opposition, 1933–34

From 30 January 1933, Hitler was chancellor of Germany but his power was limited.

- The Weimar constitution controlled what the chancellor could do.
- Hindenburg retained all the powers of the president.
- Hitler's cabinet of 11 ministers had only two other NSDAP members.
- NSDAP members numbered only about one-third of the *Reichstag*.

But within two or three years, Hitler had removed almost all opposition to his power and made himself dictator of Germany. His seven steps to total power are shown below.

Hitler's steps to total power

7. Taking the powers of the president
6. The Night of the Long Knives
5. Control of local government
4. Ban on other political parties
3. Ban on trade unions
2. The Enabling Act
1. *Reichstag* fire and 1933 elections

The Reichstag fire and the 1933 elections

In February 1933, the *Reichstag* building was destroyed by fire. A young Dutch communist supporter, Marinus van der Lubbe, was caught on the site. He confessed, was put on trial, found guilty and executed.

But van der Lubbe's execution was not enough for Hitler. He said that van der Lubbe was part of a communist conspiracy and persuaded Hindenburg to declare a state of emergency. He could now legally use decrees to govern Germany. Then he asked Hindenburg to call an election for 5 March 1933. He hoped for more Nazi seats in the *Reichstag*.

To help his election campaign, Hitler:

- raised millions of marks from rich businessmen
- used a decree to imprison political opponents and ban their newspapers
- used the SA to attack political opponents and ordered the police to turn a blind eye.

It was a bloody election campaign – violent clashes led to 70 deaths – but it worked for Hitler. The Nazis increased their *Reichstag* members to 288.

Hitler used his emergency powers to ban the communists from taking up their 81 seats. With the support of the other nationalist parties, this gave Hitler a two-thirds majority in the *Reichstag*. This was crucial. He now had enough votes to change the constitution of the republic.

The Nazi dictatorship 1933–39

The Enabling Act

The Enabling Act changed the constitution of the Weimar Republic. Hitler forced it through the *Reichstag* in late March 1933. It gave Hitler the right to make laws for four years without the consent of the *Reichstag*. It was renewed in 1937.

The new law was passed by 444 votes to 94. In this sense, it was legal – even though *Reichstag* members were intimidated during the vote. In effect, it marked the end of democratic rule and of the Weimar Republic.

Source A: This is a quotation from an observer, Sir John Wheeler-Bennet, recalling the debate on the Enabling Act.

> The Kroll Opera House, where the *Reichstag* met since … [the]…fire, was packed. There were nearly 300 Nazi deputies and 50 or so Nationalist. There was a marked absence of Communists…[and] Social Democrats… because some were in hospital, the victims of electoral violence; some had fled the country – and who could blame them?
>
> Along the corridors, SS men, in their sinister black and silver uniforms, had been posted; their legs apart and arms crossed, their eyes fixed and cruel. Outside, a mob of SA chanted threatening slogans: 'Give us the Bill or else fire and murder'.

Passing the Enabling Act gave Hitler the powers to take his next three steps to total power.

Trade unions

Trade unions were potential sources of opposition to Hitler. If communists among working men were able to control their trade unions, they could use strikes to attack the government. So, in May 1933, Hitler used his new powers to ban trade unions and make strikes illegal.

Political parties

In July 1933, Hitler issued another decree. This one (see Source C) made all political parties in Germany illegal, except for the NSDAP.

Local government

The next step was for Hitler to strengthen the central government in Berlin – which he controlled – and to weaken local government.

Under the Weimar Constitution, all regions (Länder) of Germany had their own parliament, which ran local government in the area. But in January 1934, Hitler abolished the Länder parliaments and declared that governors, appointed by him, would run every region of Germany.

Source B: A British cartoon from July 1933. President Hindenburg holds up Hitler's hand in triumph and Hermann Goering, the Nazi chief of police, removes a heavy swastika from within Hitler's glove. The people chant Hitler's name while German liberties slump, stunned and chained, in the corner.

Source C: Law against the Establishment of Parties, 14 July 1933.

> Article I: The National Socialist German Workers' Party constitutes the only political party in Germany.

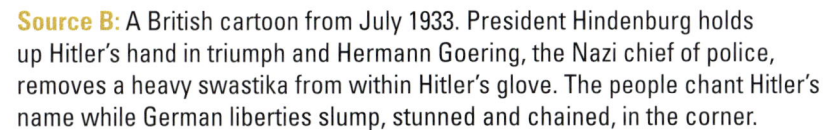

Part A: Carry out a historical enquiry

The Night of the Long Knives

By the start of 1934, Hitler had made Germany a **one-party state**. He now made sure that he was in total control of that one party – the Nazi Party.

> **One-party state:** a state where only one political party is allowed to govern.

Hitler feared Ernst Röhm, the leader of the SA.

- Röhm had merged an army veterans group, the *Stahlhelm*, with the SA. This brought SA numbers to three million. With so many SA members loyal to him, Röhm was in an ideal position to challenge Hitler.
- Röhm also opposed Hitler's policies. He criticised Hitler's links with rich industrialists and army generals. He wanted more socialist policies, to tax the rich and help the working classes.

The German Army also worried about the power of Röhm. After the Versailles Treaty the army had only 100,000 men; it was dwarfed by the SA. Röhm wanted the SA to replace the German Army.

Leaders of the SS, like Himmler and Heydrich, resented Röhm too. They wanted to reduce the power of the SA, so that they could increase their own power and the status of the SS.

In 1934, leaders of the SS and the army warned Hitler that Röhm was planning to seize power. So, on 30 June 1934, Hitler arranged for Röhm and several other senior officers of the SA to be arrested, imprisoned and shot. This is known as the Night of the Long Knives.

ResultsPlus
Top Tip

The best candidates are very specific about the two sides in the Night of the Long Knives. So make sure you are clear that:
- the SS and the Army supported it
- the SA and Hitler's political rivals, like von Schleicher, were the victims.

Events of the Night of the Long Knives

Source D: An extract from the diary of Alfred Rosenberg, a leading Nazi politician, for 30 June 1934.

> With an SS escort, the Führer knocked gently on Röhm's door: 'A message from Munich', he said in a disguised voice. 'Come in,' Röhm shouted, 'the door is open.' Hitler tore open the door, fell on Röhm as he lay in bed, grabbed him by the throat and screamed, 'You are under arrest, you pig!' Then he turned him over to the SS.

↓

Röhm was taken to Stadelheim Gaol, where, on 1 July, an SS brigade leader arrived. He left a loaded pistol, with one bullet, in Röhm's cell, thereby inviting Röhm to commit suicide. After 15 minutes, hearing no sound, he entered the cell with his deputy, where they both shot him. In addition to Röhm, six other SA leaders were shot, on Hitler's orders, at Stadelheim.

↓

In the middle of all this, Papen, still vice-chancellor, protested to Goering. He was told that the SS had things under control and he should return home for his own safety. SS squads were rounding up suspects; one group reached Papen's office before he did, shot his press secretary and arrested his staff. Papen's home was surrounded and his telephone cut off – so much for having 'Hitler in his pocket'.

↓

Over a period of about four days, about 400 people, including 150 senior members of the SA, were shot without trial. These included:
- General von Schleicher – the ex-chancellor – who was gunned down along with his wife. Goering announced they had been shot resisting arrest
- Gregor Strasser, a Nazi leader with socialist views similar to those of Röhm, who was locked in a Gestapo cell before gunmen sprayed bullets through a window. A lone gunman entered to finish him off.

The Nazi dictatorship 1933–39

Hitler was now clearly acting illegally by murdering his rivals for power. He claimed to be doing this in the interests of Germany. Some Germans objected to the violence, but few knew how terrible it had been. Most were grateful that the SA, hated for their brutality, had been restrained.

The SA continued after 1934 but it was limited to giving muscle to the Nazi Party and no longer rivalled the army. It was also now firmly under Hitler's control.

Source E: An extract from a speech Hitler made to the *Reichstag* on 13 July 1934.

> I ordered the leaders of the guilty to be shot. If anyone asks why I did not use the courts of justice, I say this: in this hour, I was responsible for the fate of the German people and I became the supreme judge of the German people.

Source F: The cover of a French magazine from August 1934. Hitler is shown, bathed in blood, dagger drawn, with dead SA storm troopers all around him. The caption says 'The Butcher of Berlin'.

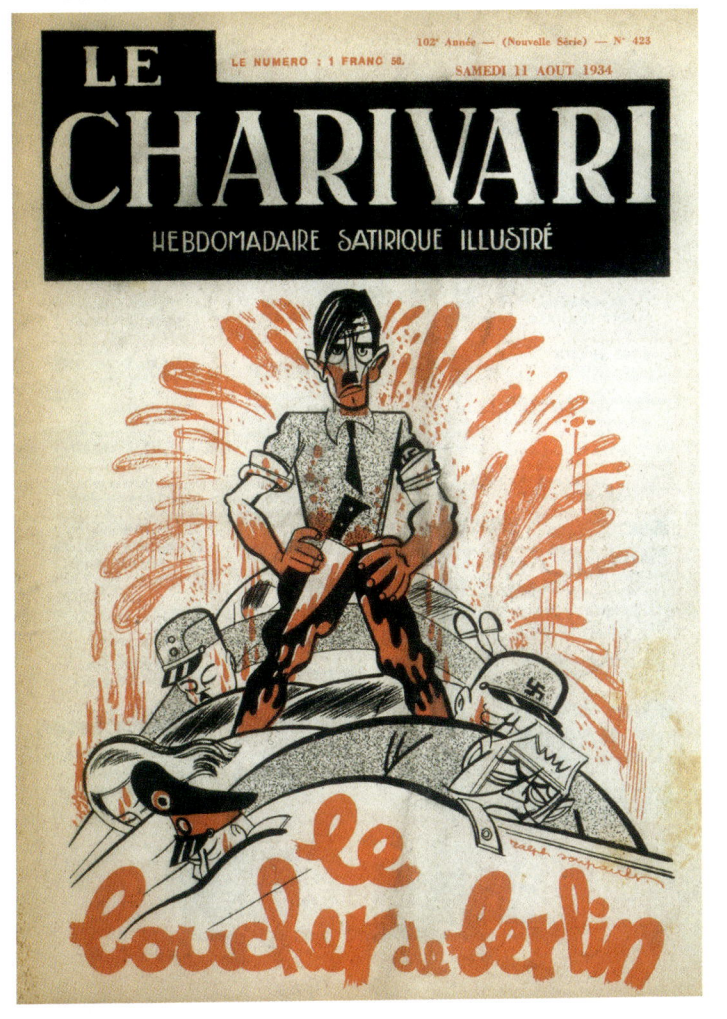

The death of President Hindenburg

On 2 August 1934, President Hindenburg died. Hitler moved in to take over supreme power.

- He declared himself Germany's Führer.
- He said that, as Führer, he would add all the president's powers to his own as chancellor.
- He demanded that every soldier in the army should swear an oath of loyalty to him.

A **plebiscite** was organised to confirm Hitler as the Führer. Bombarded by pro-Nazi propaganda, 90 per cent of voters decided in favour. The Weimar Republic had ended; Hitler's Third **Reich** had begun.

Plebiscite: a public vote.
Reich: a German word used to signify the German *State* or German *nation*.

Activity

2. For this activity, use the table of legal and illegal actions taken by Hitler which you started on page 26.
   - Imagine that Hitler is in court. The charge is that: *'Between the months of January and July 1933, Adolf Hitler illegally seized power in Germany.'*
   - Write a speech, telling the jury Hitler was guilty.
   - Now write one saying he was innocent.
   - Overall, what do you think the verdict should be?

Follow up your enquiry

Find out more about how Hitler created a dictatorship in Germany in the 1930s. Use books and the internet. For example, go to www.pearsonhotlinks.co.uk, insert the express code 8781P and then click on 'Dictatorship in Germany'.

In particular, ask yourself whether Hitler acted alone in creating a dictatorship, or was he helped by others, for example Hindenburg, rich businessmen and other nationalist parties.

Then make an ideas map to show the help he had.

Part A: Carry out a historical enquiry

Using a police state to keep control

We have seen how Hitler *took* control of Germany. The next four pages begin to show how he *kept* control of Germany. Read pages 30–33 and then do the activities at the bottom of page 33.

Hitler made Nazi Germany into a police state. This is a state in which the government uses the police – sometimes secret police – to control people's lives. Views opposed to the Nazis were suppressed using several means.

The SS

The SS (*Schutzstaffel*) was a military group, set up in 1925 as a personal bodyguard for Hitler (see pages 20–21). From 1929 it was run by Heinrich Himmler.

The main role of the SS was to be the Nazi Party's own private police force. They were totally loyal to Hitler. It was the SS who warned him about Röhm in 1934 and Hitler used SS officers to murder SA leaders during the Night of the Long Knives.

Gradually, during the 1930s, the SS was expanded to 50,000 men and put in charge of all the other state security services.

Another role of the SS was to carry out the Nazi policy of racial purification (see pages 42–43). One part of the SS was the *Totenkopf* (Death's Head units), who ran concentration camps.

Himmler was careful about recruitment to the SS. He ensured that members were Aryan in appearance; they were expected to marry 'racially pure' wives.

ResultsPlus Watch out

Many students confuse the SS with the SA.
The SA (*Sturmabteilung*) was founded in 1921. They were the brownshirts or stormtroopers who acted as the Nazi Party's private army. They were often used to protect Nazi leaders or attack Nazi rivals. Their leader, before the Night of the Long Knives, in 1934, was Ernst Röhm.

The Gestapo

The Gestapo (*Geheime Staatspolizei*) was Hitler's non-uniformed secret police force.

It was set up in 1933 by Hermann Goering and placed under the control of the SS in 1934. The Gestapo was led by Reinhard Heydrich. Germans particularly feared the Gestapo because they were not in military uniform. They could not tell them apart from other members of the public. The Gestapo arrested people who acted against or spoke out in any way against Nazi ideas. Offenders could be imprisoned without trial.

All states have police forces. But in most states the police have to act within the law and can be held to account in the courts. However, the SS and Gestapo could arrest people without being responsible to anyone but their own commanders and Hitler.

By 1939, the SS and Gestapo had put 150,000 people 'under protective arrest' in prisons. This means that they had not committed criminal acts, like stealing. They were just locked up for doing things that the Nazis disapproved of, such as voicing views opposed to Hitler and the Nazis. Many were held in concentration camps.

Source G: Werner Best, deputy head of the Gestapo.

> To discover the enemies of the state, watch them and render them harmless at the right moment…In order to fulfil this duty, the political police must be free to use every means suited to achieve the desired end.

The first Nazi concentration camp was opened at Dachau in 1933. Later that year, the first camp for women was opened at Moringen.

Concentration camps

Camps were located in isolated areas away from public gaze. They were secretive places, not controlled by normal prison rules.

Inmates were mainly political prisoners or 'undesirables', like prostitutes or minority groups, such as Jews. The SS used camp inmates as forced labour, for example producing army uniforms.

By 1939, 20,000 people were held in six concentration camps. After 1939, concentration camps grew in number and size and were used for the mass murder of minority groups, like the Jews.

The law courts

Finally, Hitler took control of the courts. He set up the National Socialist League for the Maintenance of the Law.

All judges had to be members. If any upset the Nazis, they lost their membership and could no longer be a judge.

He also set up a new People's Court, to hear treason cases – offences against the state. Judges for this court were hand picked. Even then, if Hitler thought sentences too soft, he increased them.

Source H: This banner reads 'We don't like sabotage of the work of the Führer'. It shows what the Nazis would not accept – whispered criticisms and a Jew being baptised as a Christian.

Source I: An extract from *Concentration Camp Dachau: 1933–1945* by Barbara Distel and Ruth Jakusch (1978).

> Physical punishment consisted of whipping, frequent kicking (in the abdomen or groin), slaps in the face, shooting or wounding with the bayonet. Prisoners were forced to stare for hours into glaring lights, to kneel for hours and so on.

Source J: An extract from a letter sent from Hitler's private office.

> The enclosed newspaper clipping about the conviction of the Jew Markus Luftgas to a prison sentence of two-and-a-half years has been submitted to the Führer. The Führer wishes that Luftgas be sentenced to death.

Activities

3. Use other books and the internet to do further research on concentration camps. For example, go to www.pearsonhotlinks.co.uk, insert the express code 8781P and then click on 'Concentration camps'.

4. Now put yourself in the place of a prisoner in a concentration camp in the 1930s. Write a letter to smuggle out of the camp. In the letter describe your arrest, treatment and experiences. The letter should be based on fact, not just imagination.

Part A: Carry out a historical enquiry

Hitler's treatment of the Christian churches is another example of the way in which the Nazi state controlled the German people.

The Nazis glorified strength and violence, and taught racial superiority; Christianity preaches tolerance, peace and respect for all people. This was bound to cause tension.

At first, Hitler tried to work with the Christian churches. (See Source K.) But it was cooperation on his terms. Source L may give us a better view of his intentions.

Source K: An extract from a speech by Hitler in the *Reichstag* on the Enabling Act (March 1933).

> Christianity is the unshakeable foundation of the moral and ethical life of our people. The National Government's concern will be for co-operation of the Church with the State. It expects, however, that [this] will meet with similar appreciation from their side.

The Catholic Church

In July 1933, Hitler reached a concordat (agreement) with the Pope. Hitler agreed:

- to allow freedom of worship for Catholics
- to allow Catholic schools in Germany.

The Roman Catholic Church:

- agreed that its priests would not interfere in politics
- ordered German bishops to swear loyalty to the National Socialist regime.

But Hitler didn't keep his promise to the Catholic Church. As the 1930s went on: priests were harassed; many were arrested and sent to concentration camps; Catholic schools were brought in line with state schools or closed; Catholic youth activities, like the Catholic Youth League, were banned.

By 1937, Pope Pius XI realised that the concordat was worthless. He condemned the Nazi regime in a statement known as 'With Burning Anxiety'.

Source L: A Nazi poster from 1933 shows the swastika knocking out the Catholics and the communists.

The Protestant Church

At first, many Protestants were glad to see Hitler in power. It saved them from the anti-Christian communists. These Protestants formed the German Christian Movement. Its leader was Ludwig Müller. Hitler made Müller the Reich bishop of Germany in September 1933. They allowed Nazi flags to be displayed inside their churches. Protestant pastors who supported Hitler were allowed to carry on with their church services as normal.

However, many Protestant Christians came to oppose Hitler's policies. Some even spoke out against him. The most famous of these was Pastor Martin Niemöller. In 1933, Niemöller was one of the Protestant pastors who set up the Pastors' Emergency League (PEL). These Protestants campaigned against Nazi actions. They became troublesome to Hitler – and paid the price in Hitler's police state. Many were arrested and imprisoned. In 1937, Niemöller was sent to a concentration camp.

Activity

5. Write down three things on this page which suggest that Hitler wanted cooperation with the churches and three points which suggest he did not. What do you think? Did Hitler want to cooperate with the churches or not?

The Nazi dictatorship 1933–39

In Hitler's police state, **censorship** was another way of controlling people. It controlled their ideas and opinions. Hitler put Joseph Goebbels in charge of the Ministry of Public Enlightenment and Propaganda. This banned other people's political opinions as well as artistic and cultural views of which Hitler disapproved.

The press

Newspapers were encouraged by the Nazis – but they had to provide views which the Nazis agreed with or face the consequences. Journalists were given regular briefings, containing the information the government was willing to publicise; they were sometimes given direct instructions as to what to write.

Under these circumstances, there could be no free press in Germany; every newspaper was a Nazi newspaper.

Universities

The Nazis had little respect for academic research. The Nazi Education Minister once said 'A road-sweeper sweeps 1,000 microbes with a stroke; a scientist preens himself on discovering a single microbe.' Between 1933 and 1938, 3,000 professors or lecturers were dismissed from jobs.

Research was heavily directed by the ministry and the results were expected to support Nazi views. All academics who remained had to agree publicly to things which were clearly nonsense (see Source N).

The arts

The Nazis controlled the supply of books. Millions of books they didn't agree with were taken from libraries and burned on huge bonfires. On one occasion, students in Berlin burned 20,000 books written by Jews, communists and anti-Nazi authors.

Music was also censored. Jazz music was banned; it was seen as black music and therefore inferior. Mendelssohn's work was also banned because he was partly Jewish.

Wagner was promoted because he put to music heroic German legends from the past. Traditional German folk music was also favoured.

In the theatre, plays about German history and politics were supported as long as they reflected Nazi views.

Source M: A Ministry of Propaganda order, 1935.

> Photos showing members of the Reich government at dining tables in front of rows of bottles must not be published in future. This has given the absurd impression that members of the government are living it up.

Source N: A quotation from the Director of the Institute of Physics, in Dresden.

> Physics is the creation of the German mind…In fact, all European science comes from Aryan thought.

Censorship: banning views or information which you do not want people to see.

ResultsPlus Watch out

Some students confuse Goering with Goebbels.
- Hermann Goering was Hitler's chief of police
- Joseph Goebbels was Hitler's minister for censorship and propaganda.

Activity

6. Based on information on pages 30–33, draw a diagram to represent Hitler's police state.
   - You might draw a spider's web, with Hitler at the centre and the web made up the Gestapo, censorship, etc.
   - You might draw the German people trapped behind bars, with the bars representing the SS, concentration camps, etc.

   But don't just copy one of these ideas. Read pages 30–33 and think of your own diagram.

   Then write a sentence saying how your diagram gives a good picture of Hitler's police state.

Part A: Carry out a historical enquiry

Propaganda

The Nazis used propaganda to spread their ideas and to strengthen their hold on power. This propaganda took many forms, but these were all controlled by Joseph Goebbels, Hitler's Minister of Public Enlightenment and Propaganda.

Source O: This American cartoon, from 1938, shows Goebbels as the ringmaster of the Nazi propaganda circus.

Political campaigns

By 1933, the Nazis were very experienced in using propaganda in political campaigns (see page 20). This continued during the 1930s. For example:

- Government posters were used to advertise Nazi views.
- Goebbels expanded his use of rallies and parades. A mass rally was held each year at Nuremberg to create a sense of German unity and advertise the strength of the Nazi Party.
- Aeroplanes were used to transport Hitler quickly from place to place, so that he could be seen in person by millions of Germans.

Source P: An extract from *Adolf Hitler* by John Toland, 1976, describing the 1934 Nuremberg Rally.

> Crowning the stadium was a giant eagle with a 100-foot wing-spread, thousands of swastika banners and 130 anti-aircraft searchlights with a range of 25,000 feet.
>
> When 200,000 Party faithful, with 20,000 flags crowded in, the effects of gleaming searchlight pillars was breathtaking. Hitler's voice came across the field with eerie effect.

Radio

Goebbels started to use the power of the radio.

- All radio stations were put under Nazi control.
- Hitler and other Nazi officials made frequent broadcasts.
- Cheap mass-produced radios were sold or placed in cafes, factories and schools; speakers were even placed in the street.
- By the 1930s there were more radios per person in Germany than anywhere else in Europe.

Source Q: A Ministry of Propaganda order, March 1934.

> Attention! On Wednesday 21st March, the Führer is speaking on all German (radio) stations from 11am to 11.50am… All factory owners, stores, offices, shops, pubs and flats must put up speakers an hour before, so that the whole workforce can hear.

Cinema

Goebbels also influenced films at cinemas. With audiences of over 250 million in 1933, films had excellent potential for getting Nazi views across.

- Films were shown alongside a 45-minute official newsreel, publicising Germany's achievements.
- From 1934, film-makers had to send the plot of every new film to Goebbels for approval.
- Some films had overtly political messages, like *Hitlerjunge Quex* (1933), in which a young member of the Nazi party was killed by communists.

Did you know?

Hitler and Goebbels noticed the popularity of Mickey Mouse films so they had a propaganda cartoon made. The leading character, Hansi, was a canary, with three fingers in white gloves, just like Mickey, but with Hitler's lick of hair across his forehead. In the film, Hansi was pestered by villainous black crows with Jewish features.

Sport

HItler also used sport to show Nazi Germany in a good light. His best chance to do this was in 1936, when the Olympic Games were held in Berlin.

- The Nazis built an Olympic stadium which could hold 110,000 people and was the largest in the world, to reflect the power of Germany.
- All the events were faultlessly organised, to show off German efficiency.
- Germany won 33 gold medals, more than any other country – and more silver and bronze too. Hitler said this proved Aryan superiority.

Did you know?

Gretel Bergmann was the women's high-jump champion for Germany. She was in the Olympic team, but she was Jewish. The Germans also picked another German high jumper, Dora Ratjen, who beat Gretel. Later, Dora Ratjen was found to be a man – a member of the Hitler Youth, picked to ensure that a Jewish German woman could not win a gold medal.

Hitler the figurehead

A key feature of Nazi propaganda was Hitler himself.

National Socialism depended upon loyalty to one national leader, who would be trusted to act in the best interests of the whole nation. So Hitler's image was carefully crafted. He was the one who united the nation.

He was shown as strong and decisive. But he was also frequently pictured with children to show that he was a caring father figure.

Activity

7. Source O describes Goebbels as the ringmaster of the Nazi circus. Think about the word 'ringmaster'. Look it up in a dictionary if that helps. Also think about the way that Goebbels used:

   - censorship
   - propaganda.

   Now write a paragraph to explain why the word 'ringmaster' is a good word for what he did.

Your conclusion so far

During this section of the book, covering the Nazi dictatorship, we have seen how the Nazis:

- *took* total control of Germany 1933–34
- *kept* control of Germany 1933–39.

As a result of all this, some people call Nazi Germany a *totalitarian* state – where the state, ruled by a dictator, controls all aspects of national life.

Look back at pages 26–35 on the Nazi dictatorship and list all the ways in which Nazi Germany had become a totalitarian state.

When you have finished, go to www.pearsonhotlinks.co.uk, insert the express code 8781P and then click on 'Totalitarian state'.

How did you do? Did you make a better case than the one on the internet?

Part A: Carry out a historical enquiry

A4 Key features of Nazi rule 1933–39

Learning outcomes
By the end of this topic, you should be able to understand what happened between 1933 and 1939 in Nazi Germany to:
- young people and women
- work, employment and the standard of living
- minority groups.

Youth and education in Nazi Germany

Nazis had very different ideas about boys and girls.

- They wanted boys to do paid work and be in the military.
- Girls were intended to be good wives and mothers.

This shaped all Nazi policies towards German children.

Schools

All children attended school until they were 14 years old. After that, school was voluntary.

Teachers had to swear an oath of loyalty to Hitler and join the Nazi Teachers' League. They were expected to pass on Nazi political views and decorate their classrooms with Nazi posters and flags. They taught the Nazi salute and started each lesson with the children saying 'Heil Hitler'.

New subjects were added to spread Nazi opinions.

- In Race Studies, pupils were told that Aryans were superior and that they should not marry Jews.
- *Mein Kampf* became a compulsory school text.
- Subjects like history and mathematics were used to spread Nazi political views.

Source B: A question from a German maths textbook, 1933.

> The Jews are aliens in Germany. In 1933 there were 66,060,000 people in Germany of whom 499,862 were Jews. What is the percentage of aliens in Germany?

- PE took up about one-sixth of school time, to keep young people healthy enough to work or fight for Germany.
- Boys and girls went to separate schools.
- Domestic science, including cookery and needlework, was compulsory for girls.

Source C: An extract from a report by the British Ambassador, sent to London in 1938.

> The German schoolboy is being educated, mentally and physically, to defend his country;…he will be equally fitted to march on foreign soil.

Source A: A photograph of a teacher and children at a German school in 1935.

Key features of Nazi rule 1933–39

Youth movements

Outside school, the Nazi government ran a series of youth movements.

- Boys started, aged 6, in the *Pimpfen* (Little Fellows) and did camping and hiking.
- When they reached 14, they could join the *Hitler Jugend* (Hitler Youth), which did military training, just like the SA.
- Girls were in separate groups, such as the League of German Maidens. Girls had training for health and motherhood.

By 1939, there were 8 million boys in the Hitler Youth, so its impact on German society was huge.

Source D: A 1935 poster for the League of German Maidens. Note the Aryan girl, her look of confidence and the Nazi flags.

However, the breezy posters and massed rallies don't show the full story. In 1938, there were 3 million boys who had not joined Hitler Youth. Many others attended half-heartedly.

Some youngsters even joined rival groups, who found simple ways to rebel. They grew their hair long or listened to modern swing music. Their groups were often mixed-sex groups. They sometimes daubed anti-Nazi slogans on walls.

The most well known of these groups was the Edelweiss Pirates. It had about 2,000 members by 1939.

Follow up your enquiry

1. Find out more about the Edelweiss Pirates. For example, go to www.pearsonhotlinks.co.uk, insert the express code 8781P and then click on 'Edelweiss Pirates' to listen to two interviews with an ex-member of the group.
2. Based on the interviews, answer these questions:
   - How serious were the 'crimes' committed by the Edelweiss Pirates?
   - How serious to Walter Mayer were the consequences of being an Edelweiss Pirate?

Activities

1. To investigate the aims of Nazi policies towards young people, make a table with the following headings.

Teaching Nazi beliefs	Making Germany stronger	Treating boys and girls differently	Meeting the needs of individual children

2. Write as much information as you can about Nazi youth policy under each heading.
3. When it is finished, what does your table suggest were the aims of Nazi policies towards youth?

Part A: Carry out a historical enquiry

Women in Nazi Germany, 1933–39

During the early years of the Weimar Republic, women had gained many freedoms:

- Women over 20 years of age were given the vote and there were about 20 female members of the *Reichstag*.
- Women were also more likely to go out to work than in previous years and more likely to work in the professions, where they were often paid on an equal basis to men. For example, there were about 100,000 female teachers in Germany by 1933.
- Women also started to enjoy more social activities outside the family and express their freedom in the way they dressed.

But the Nazis had a very different view of how women should fit into society. They believed that, like Germany's youth, women should serve their society, and the best way to do this was to be good mothers. These policies towards women had the extra benefit for the Nazis of freeing up jobs for men – and thus reducing unemployment.

The Nazis also had another problem which affected women – a falling birth rate. They wanted to reverse this, so the Nazis developed further policies to encourage marriage and childbirth.

NAZI BELIEFS ABOUT WOMEN
To be good mothers, German women should:

- stay healthy; have children; raise them as good Germans
- never wear make-up or dye or perm their hair
- learn housecraft – cookery and needlework
- marry and enable their husbands to be useful workers
- stay at home with domestic matters, not work or politics

NAZI POLICIES ABOUT WOMEN
Nazi beliefs about women shaped Nazi policies toward them:

- The German Women's Enterprise was formed to arrange classes and radio broadcasts, teaching good motherhood.
- Women were encouraged to leave work and concentrate on the 3Ks – *Kinder, Küche, Kirche* (children, kitchen and church).
- Some professional women were forced to leave their well-paid jobs as doctors, lawyers or teachers.
- In 1933, the Law for the Encouragement of Marriage was introduced. Loans of 1,000 marks, worth about nine months' wages, were provided for young couples to marry, as long as the wife left work. For each one of their first four children, the couple could keep a quarter of the loan. There were other payments to encourage childbirth too.
- The Mother's Cross was an award given to women for the number of children they had: bronze for four or five children, silver for six or seven children, and gold for eight or more. Medals were presented each year on Hitler's mother's birthday.

Key features of Nazi rule 1933–39

ResultsPlus
Watch out

Don't say Hitler thought women were inferior. He thought women were different and should be treated differently. But he considered women's roles to be very important. However, many Germans disagreed with Hitler's view of women.

Source E: A quotation from Wilhelmine Haferkamp, who was 22 years old in 1933.

> I got 30 marks per child from the Hitler government and 20 marks from the city. That was a lot of money. I sometimes got more 'child money' than my husband earned.

Source F: Wilhelmine Haferkamp eventually had ten children. This is another quotation from her.

> I was proud. When I got the gold, there was a big celebration in a school, where the mothers were all invited for coffee and cake.

By about 1938, German industry needed more women workers, so some of these policies were relaxed. Nevertheless, fewer women were working in Germany in 1939 than in the early 1920s.

Hitler believed that these policies were fair to women. In 1935, he said: 'Both sexes have their tasks. These tasks are equal in dignity and value.'

But there was a good deal of opposition to Nazi policies towards women. Other political parties tried to take advantage of this (see Source H). Some women said that the Nazi view of women encouraged men to see women as inferior.

Source G: An extract from a letter to a Leipzig newspaper in 1934

> A son, even the youngest, laughs in his mother's face. He regards her as his servant and women in general are merely willing tools of his aims.

Follow up your enquiry

1. *Lebensborn* was another Nazi policy to boost childbirth. Use books and the internet to find out about it. For example, go to www.pearsonhotlinks.co.uk, insert the express code 8781P and then click on 'Lebensborn' to watch a video from the Jewish Library.
2. Try to find a link between *Lebensborn* and the pop group Abba.

Activity

4. Identify one Nazi belief about the role of women. Then find a Nazi policy about women which was based on that belief.
   Try to do this three times.

Source H: A Social Democrat poster showing a woman downtrodden by an unfeeling Nazi.

FRAUEN, so geht's euch im »Dritten Reich«!

»Die Frau muß wieder Magd und Dienerin werden« sagt der Naziführer Feder. Deshalb ist auch in der Hakenkreuzfraktion keine Frau vertreten.

Eure Antwort: Kampf den Nazi – – für die Sozialdemokratie!

Part A: Carry out a historical enquiry

Economic policy, 1933–39

The Nazis also made every aspect of the economy serve the needs of the state:

Workers

Hitler believed that workers should be organised to benefit the state.

He could see that powerful trade unions could disrupt the economy, so he banned trade unions in 1933. Instead, Hitler set up the DAF (German Labour Front).

The DAF had the power, in all factories, mines, munitions plants and shipyards, to decide workers':

- employment rights
- working hours
- rates of pay
- punishments for indiscipline.

The needs of the state

Trade

The Nazis also believed that trade should be used to benefit the state. Hitler knew that, if Germany relied upon rival powers for imports, this made Germany weaker. So Hitler adopted an economic policy called 'autarky'. This means making a country self-sufficient, so that it doesn't rely upon other, rival countries.

Dr Hjalmar Schacht was the German Minister for the Economy from 1934. He negotiated trade deals with a small number of friendly countries. These provided Germany with raw materials; in exchange, Germany provided them with manufactured goods.

German production increased by 50 per cent between 1933 and 1935 and Germany had a small trading surplus.

The unemployed

Hitler also believed that the unemployed should be made to benefit the state. Too many unemployed men were dangerous, because:

- unemployed workers often supported the communists, Hitler's rivals
- the unemployed sapped the strength of a nation. Men needed to be put to useful work.

So, in 1934 the Nazis set up the RAD (National Labour Service). The RAD provided manual work for the unemployed.

At first it was a voluntary scheme, but from 1935 it was made compulsory for all young men to serve for six months in the RAD.

The RAD was organised like an army. Workers wore uniforms, lived in camps and did military drill and parades as well as work. Rates of pay were very low and some complained of very poor food.

Those in the RAD worked in the fields and built public buildings and *Autobahnen* (motorways).

These projects were also good for Germany. By 1939, Germany had 7,000 miles of autobahn.

Rearmament

Hitler also used German industry to serve the needs of the state.

The Nazis believed Germany needed to be a strong military power so that it could stand up against its rivals and press for *Lebensraum* – living space for the German people.

So the Nazis boosted the army; it numbered about:

- 100,000 in 1933
- 500,000 in 1936
- 900,000 in 1939.

This meant that German industry was given the essential task of equipping the nation's army. It provided a huge volume of uniforms, equipment and arms. For example from 1933 to 1939:

- the value of arms it supplied to the government rose from 3.5 billion marks to 26 billion marks
- the volume of iron and steel trebled
- production of plastic increased by 460 per cent.

Key features of Nazi rule 1933–39

The standard of living, 1933–39

The Nazi economy was organised to benefit the state. But Hitler knew that his economic changes had to benefit people too – his political survival could depend upon it. So the German people clearly benefited in some ways from Nazi economic policies – but in other ways, the benefits were less clear.

The German people benefited	Did they really?
Unemployment fell. • It was 4.8 million in 1933 and 0.4 million in 1938. • More families were enjoying the benefits of a regular income.	• Many of the employed were in the military rather than productive jobs – or they were doing compulsory work for the RAD in very poor conditions. • Some of the extra jobs for men had only been achieved by moving women and Jews out of jobs.
Wage levels also improved. • Compared to 1933 levels, wages rose by 20% by 1938.	• But rising prices cancelled out wage increases. Food prices rose by 20% in Germany between 1933 and 1939. This was because the Nazis limited farm output in order to keep farmers' incomes high.
People could afford to buy more. • Compared to 1933 levels, sales rose 45% by 1938. **Luxury goods increased.** • Car ownership trebled in Germany in the 1930s.	• During the depression of 1929 to 1933, standards of living were very low, so any improvements measured against 1933 were really just a return to normal. • Cars were quite new. Ownership grew rapidly in many other western countries too.
The Nazis started the *Schönheit der Arbeit* (SdA) – Beauty of Labour. • This organisation tried to ensure good standards at work – of safety, cleanliness, lighting, noise levels, ventilation – and hot meals.	• But with trade unions banned, workers' freedoms had been reduced and their working hours had increased – on average from 43 hours a week to 49 hours.
The Nazis started the *Kraft durch Freude* (KdF) – Strength through Joy. • This provided leisure activities for workers, including sports facilities, films, outings and theatre shows. KdF became the world's largest tour operator of the 1930s.	• Only a minority of workers could actually afford the activities and holidays provided by Strength through Joy.

It's doubtful that Hitler's economic policies would have worked in the long term. After 1936, rearmament meant that:

- the government was spending more than its income from taxes
- imports were bigger than exports.

Like people, countries can't go on spending more than they earn.

> ### Activity
>
> 5. List three ways in which Germany benefited from Hitler's economic policies.
>
>   List three ways in which German people benefited from Hitler's economic policies.
>
>   Who benefited more, the German state or the German people?

Part A: Carry out a historical enquiry

Persecution of minorities, 1933–39

Many minority groups were badly treated in Nazi Germany. They included vagrants, homosexuals, Gypsies, the disabled and, most infamously, Jews.

Anti-Semitism: the background

Anti-Jewish views, often referred to as anti-Semitism, had long been common in Europe.

- Some Christians hated Jews, blaming them for the execution of Christ.
- When times were hard, people often look for scapegoats. Many Germans wrongly blamed the Jews for defeat in the First World War.
- The Jews' religion, customs and looks made them stand out as 'different', making it easier for racists to pick on them.

Among many, Hitler was one who blamed Germany's problems on the Jews.

Source I: A quotation from Hitler, speaking to an acquaintance, Josef Hell, in 1922.

> If ever in power, the end of the Jews will be my first job. I shall have gallows built in Munich. Then Jews will be hanged, and will stay hanging till they stink… Then the same in other cities till Germany is cleansed of the last Jew.

In 1925, Hitler set out his racial views more clearly in *Mein Kampf*. He described a hierarchy of races.

- The Aryan race was the superior race – the *Herrenvolk* or master race. They were portrayed as tall, blond, blue-eyed and athletic.
- Other people belonged to lesser races.
- Then there were the *Untermenschen*, or subhumans.
- Worst of the *Untermenschen*, according to Hitler, were Gypsies and Jews. Hitler called them *Lebensunwertes*, meaning they were unworthy of life.

Activity

6. There are many dates and events in this chapter. To help you to visualise these events, make a timeline from **1933 to 1939**.
   - Above the line, record events about the **persecution** of Jews.
   - Below the line, record events about the persecution of other minority groups.

Persecution: systematic mistreatment of an individual or group of people.

Persecution starts

When the Nazis first came to power, their persecution of Jews was limited.

- From April 1933, there were Nazi boycotts of Jewish businesses.
- From September 1933, Jews were banned from inheriting land.
- In May 1935, Jews were banned from the army.
- From June 1935, Jews were banned from restaurants.

Source J: A photograph of the Nazi boycott of Jewish businesses in 1933. The SA put posters on the windows of Jewish shops telling people not to go in. Then they stood outside to intimidate shoppers.

The Nuremberg Laws

Persecution then became worse. The **Nuremberg Laws** were passed in September 1935. These said Jews:

- could no longer vote, hold government office or have German passports
- had separate areas on buses and trains
- could not marry German citizens.

Kristallnacht

In November 1938, a young Polish Jew, Herschel Grynszpan, shot and killed an official at the German embassy in Paris. He was angry at the way his parents had been treated. Germans were outraged. Goebbels said Hitler had ordered that, if Germans took revenge on the Jews, the police should do nothing about it. On 9 November, gangs attacked Jews and their property. Official figures listed 814 shops, 171 homes and 191 synagogues destroyed. About 100 Jews were killed. This was called *Kristallnacht* – the Night of Broken Glass.

The aftermath

Goebbels blamed the Jews for starting the trouble on *Kristallnacht*. Persecution then became even worse. He said that Jews would be:

- fined 1 billion marks and banned from running shops or businesses
- banned from German schools or universities.

The SA and SS also started to round up Jews as punishment. By 12 November, 20,000 Jews had been sent to concentration camps. Then, in April 1939, Jews were evicted from their homes and detained until they could be deported. They were crowded into separate areas of cities, called ghettoes. Sometimes these were fenced off. Living conditions in the ghettoes were desperately overcrowded and there were food shortages.

Did you know?

Once the Second World War started, in 1939, the persecution of Jews became even worse. It is estimated that six million Jews were murdered in concentration camps by the end of the war.

Key features of Nazi rule 1933–39

Persecution of other minorities

Nazis believed that several other racial minorities, like Gypsies, were subhuman and had no place in the German community. They suffered similar persecution to the Jews.

- After 1933, Gypsies were often arrested and sent to concentration camps.
- From 1935, the Nuremberg Laws were used against Gypsies. Marriage between Gypsies and Germans was forbidden.
- In April 1939, orders were given to collect all Gypsies within enclosed and guarded ghettos inside Germany, ready to be deported.

Nazis also persecuted people who, they believed, undermined moral standards, such as prostitutes, homosexuals, alcoholics, pacifists, beggars, hooligans and persistent criminals.

They also persecuted those who, they said, weakened the pure German bloodline, such as the unhealthy, the disabled or the mentally ill.

- In 1933, a law was passed allowing people to be sterilised. This was used for people with learning difficulties, the physically or mentally disabled and alcoholics. Between 1934 and 1945, 700,000 Germans were sterilised.
- Some Germans believed that, from 1933, there was an unofficial policy to kill disabled children. A secret official policy was started in 1939. By 1945, 6,000 disabled Germans had been killed by starvation or lethal injection.

Your conclusion so far

- This section, covering key features of Nazi rule, describes Nazi policies on young people, women, the economy and minority groups.
- A common theme of all these policies is that they all treated the needs of the individual as if they were less important than the needs of the state.

Demonstrate this common theme by finding an example of the way the needs of the state were placed above the individual needs of:

- young people
- women
- workers
- minority groups.

Part A: Carry out a historical enquiry

Enquiry and writing skills support

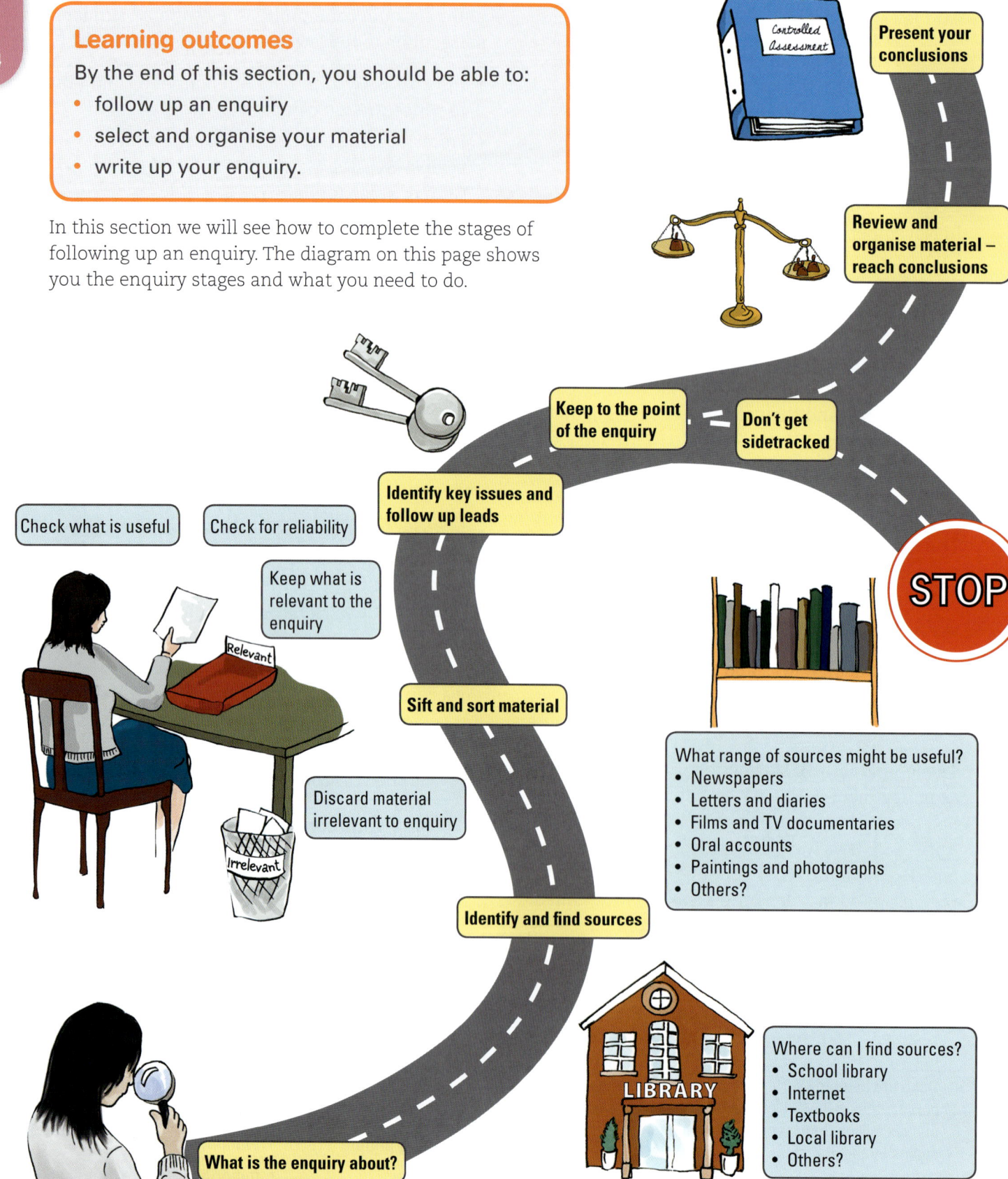

Learning outcomes

By the end of this section, you should be able to:
- follow up an enquiry
- select and organise your material
- write up your enquiry.

In this section we will see how to complete the stages of following up an enquiry. The diagram on this page shows you the enquiry stages and what you need to do.

Present your conclusions

Review and organise material – reach conclusions

Keep to the point of the enquiry

Don't get sidetracked

Identify key issues and follow up leads

Check what is useful

Check for reliability

Keep what is relevant to the enquiry

Sift and sort material

Discard material irrelevant to enquiry

What range of sources might be useful?
- Newspapers
- Letters and diaries
- Films and TV documentaries
- Oral accounts
- Paintings and photographs
- Others?

Identify and find sources

Where can I find sources?
- School library
- Internet
- Textbooks
- Local library
- Others?

What is the enquiry about?

Following up an enquiry 1: The problems facing the Weimar Republic in the years 1918–23

Your controlled assessment Part A task will be similar to this one:

> **Enquiry focus**
> Your enquiry task will focus on the reasons for the political problems facing the Weimar Republic in the years 1918–23.

In this practice we are going to follow up the enquiry focus shown above. You will be able to use the skills you develop to follow up your own Part A enquiry.

What is the enquiry about?

Your first step is to identify the precise enquiry. In this instance, it's about explaining why there were so many political problems in the 'years of crisis' for the Weimar Republic: 1918–23. This enquiry is trying to find out:

- what the different political problems were and what caused them
- how the different problems connected together.

Identify and find sources

The next stage is to gather your information. Start with an easy outline book and read through the relevant material. Write some summary notes, making sure you include the book title, author and the pages where you have found the information. You should only start to look for more in-depth information when you have used two or three textbooks which give you the basic information.

For this enquiry, begin by rereading pages 4–9 of this book and completing activities 1–3.

To add to your sources, you might start by doing a quick search on the internet but you should also look at books by historians. When you find a book, check the book contents page and the index to make sure it covers the topic you want to research. For this enquiry, you would want to look up 'Weimar Republic', 'political problems, Weimar' and '1918–23'. You could also use television documentaries as a source of information but be careful to check them against other sources to be sure they have not been too dramatised or exaggerated.

Activities

Making notes

1. Make a bullet point list of useful information from your first source of information.

   For example:

   The Weimar Constitution made it difficult for the government to act quickly and decisively.

   Both extreme left-wing and right-wing groups tried to overthrow the government.

2. Now repeat this process for two other textbooks or simple overviews.

3. Begin to organise your notes. You could sort them into a chart like the one below.

Political problem	Why was it a problem?

Sift and sort material

Go through your new sources and make additional notes. It will help if you use a fresh page for each book or other source of information. Remember that the book or the webpage you've found was not written to answer your specific question. For example, this enquiry is about explaining why the Weimar Republic faced different political problems up to 1923. You have to choose what to take from your source to address that enquiry focus – see Activity 4 on page 46 for more on this.

Identify leads to follow up. For example, Source A tells you that the Weimar Republic came under threat from both the political right and the political left, and it outlines some of the causes of this:

- Political opponents on the left thought the Weimar Republic was blocking a communist takeover.
- Political opponents on the right thought a democracy weakened Germany.

You could follow up these two leads, going through the same process of finding, sifting and sorting, and noting information.

Part A: Carry out a historical enquiry

ResultsPlus
Top Tip

Looking for information can be a slow process. You might read through a lot to get a small piece of new information. But your work is better if you concentrate on what's new and relevant, rather than adding something that repeats information you already have or is not relevant.

Stick to the enquiry path

Don't go off track! On a journey, detours and side roads can be great fun and you can follow them up just because they are interesting. Remember, though, to return to your enquiry path – and not to add in material which isn't relevant. For example, information about the Dawes Plan in 1924 wouldn't directly help you answer an enquiry about the political problems in 1918–1923.

Source A: From *Democracy and Dictatorship in Germany 1919-1963*, by Professor Mary Fulbrook and David Williamson, 2008.

> **Threats to the Weimar Republic, 1919-20**
>
> By early 1920 the authority...of the Weimar coalition was already badly damaged and it faced threats from both the Left and the Right. On the one hand, many of the workers were disappointed that their demands for the nationalisation of key industries and the formation of workers' factory councils...had come to nothing...
>
> On the other hand, the old nationalist Right, which had been shell-shocked by the events of November 1918, was re-emerging. The attitude of the army was ambiguous [not clear-cut]. While it hated the Weimar Republic, some [army] officers were ready to overthrow it; [while other officers] urged the army to [stay out of] politics and concentrate on creating a tightly-knit professional force, which could one day be expanded again. The professional classes, that is university and school teachers, judges and civil servants, etc., were also for the most part hostile to the new regime.

Activities

Selecting information

4. Read Source A and decide with a partner how much of it is useful for the enquiry. Remember:
   - You want to identify Weimar's political problems and explain why they had developed.
   - Usually you want only new points.
   - Sometimes you may want to make a note that two sources agree about an important point.

5. Photocopy or write out the whole passage. Colour code it: green for new information on political problems; yellow for information on why these problems had come about and blue for duplication – information you already know from other sources.

   Some parts have been done for you.

Using sources carefully

So far we have applied two tests when using sources – relevance and duplication. Sometimes you will also need to think about reliability. You need to be particularly careful about internet sources because they are sometimes anonymous and it is difficult to check the information they contain. Remember that many internet sites are just opinions without any factual support.

With any source, think about purpose and possible bias. As you use your sources, apply the RDR tests: Relevance, Duplication and Reliability.

Activity

Relevance and reliability

6. Study Source B. This table is from a history of socialist revolutionaries in Germany. The table was included in an article published on a Marxist website (although you will also find this table in other sources), which believes that a socialist revolution is needed to create a better society for everyone.

Enquiry and writing skills support

Activities

7. Decide with a partner which of these statements about Source B you agree with. Choose as many as you like.
   - It is not biased.
   - It is biased but still has some useful information.
   - It includes information about the political problems facing the Weimar Republic.
   - It makes statements about why the Weimar government faced threats from the extreme right and the left.
   - The information is reliable because statistics like these are usually accurate.
   - The information is not reliable because statistics are always impossible to prove.
   - Further research would be needed to decide whether the information was reliable or not.
   - It is mainly relevant to this enquiry.
   - It does not add much to this enquiry.
8. Add any useful information to your notes.

Source B: Reported in 'Germany – from Revolution to Counter-Revolution' by Rob Sewell, 1988 on the website of the International Marxist Tendency.

Political murders committed (January 1919–June 1922) by persons belonging to the right and left.

	RIGHT	LEFT
Number of political murders committed	354	22
Number of persons sentenced for these murders	24	38
Death sentences	-	10
Confessed assassins found 'Not Guilty'	23	-
Political assassins subsequently promoted in the Army	3	-
Average length of prison term per murder	4 months	15 years
Average fine per murder	2 marks	–

(Source: *Vier Jahre Politischer Mord*, E.J. Gumbel.)

Identify key issues and follow up leads

So far this enquiry has shown why the Weimar Republic faced many different political problems. We can start to group these reasons in different ways – making them easier to deal with and to discuss. We can also show how many of the problems and their causes linked together and reinforced each other.

Some political problems had causes *outside* the Republic – such as the Treaty of Versailles.

Some political problems had causes *inside* the Republic – for example the weak and fragile government.

The *left* and the *right* had very different ideas about how to solve Germany's problems – pleasing both sides was impossible.

The far left and the far right both threatened the survival of the Republic. It chose to use one side to defeat the other: it used the right to put down the left.

Activities

9. Study Source C in the source file on page 48. It gives two new leads: the reasons for weak governments but also the view that the voting system of the Republic was not necessarily a cause of Weimar's most serious political problems.
10. Add information from Source C to your notes. In your real enquiry, it will help if you add page numbers, in case you want to find the passage again.
11. Begin to organise your information under key headings whenever you use a new source.

ResultsPlus
Top Tip

Good answers to Part A questions will include well-chosen short quotations from the books they use.

Part A: Carry out a historical enquiry

Source file

Source C: An extract from *GCSE Modern World History second edition*, by Ben Walsh, 2001.

[The Spartacists] argued strongly against Ebert's [leader of the Republic] plans for a democratic Germany. They wanted a Germany ruled by workers' councils or soviets. Early in 1919 the Spartacists launched their bid for power. Joined by rebel soldiers and sailors, they set up soviets in many towns. Not all soldiers were on the side of the Spartacists, however. Some anti-Communist ex-soldiers had formed themselves into vigilante groups called Freikorps. Ebert made an agreement with the commanders of the army and the Freikorps to put down the rebellion.

Source D: An extract from *The Coming of the Third Reich* by Richard J. Evans, 2004.

[C]hanges of government in the Weimar Republic were very frequent. Between 13 February 1919 and 30 January 1933 there were no fewer than twenty different cabinets, each lasting on average 239 days, or somewhat less than eight months. Coalition governments, it was sometimes said, made for unstable government, as the different parties were constantly squabbling over personalities and policies. It also made for weak government, since all they could settle on was the lowest common denominator and the line of least resistance...

[However,] proportional representation did not, as some have claimed, encourage political anarchy and thereby facilitate the rise of the extreme right. An electoral system based on a first-past-the-post system, where the candidate who won the most votes in each constituency automatically won the seat, might have given the Nazi Party even more seats than it eventually obtained in the last elections of the Weimar Republic.

Source E: An extract from *Second Reich to Third Reich: Germany 1918-45* by Alan White, 2010.

Extremists of the left and right hated the Weimar Republic. Reconciling themselves to it was unthinkable. What they hoped to do was destroy it. In early 1919 their chances of success appeared to be remote: the extreme right had been discredited by Germany's defeat and the extreme left had been pulverised by the Free Corps. But the extremists of the right in particular soon recovered. The key to their political comeback was the Treaty of Versailles. Much harsher than expected, the Treaty provoked outrage within Germany – outrage which the extreme right was able to exploit for its own ends.

Source F: *From Hitler, a study in tyranny* by Alan Bullock, 1965.

When the war ended and the Republic was proclaimed, Hitler was still in hospital at Pasewalk. The acknowledgement of Germany's defeat and the establishment of a democratic Republic, in which the Social Democrats played the leading part, were both intolerable to him. There is no reason to doubt his statement that the shock of Germany's surrender was a decisive experience in his life. [Hitler wrote in *Mein Kampf*] 'Everything went black before my eyes as I staggered back to my ward and buried my aching head between the blankets and pillow...The following days were terrible to bear and the nights still worse... During these nights my hatred increased, hatred for the originators of this dastardly crime.'

Source G: An extract from a government proclamation during the Kapp Putsch of March 1920; the government called on workers to go out on strike to help defeat the Kapp Putsch.

Workers, Party comrades! The military putsch has started...The achievements of a whole year are to be smashed, your dearly bought freedom to be destroyed. Everything is at stake! No factory must work... Therefore, down tools! Come out on strike...Paralysis of all economic life is the only way to prevent the return of the dictatorship of Wilhelm II [this was a right wing aim].

Source H: An extract from *A Social History of the Third Reich* by Richard Grunberger, 2005.

> The courts treated right-wing terrorism with a leniency best exemplified by Hitler's one-year jail sentence after the bloodily abortive Munich putsch of November 1923...While the majority of the people actively deserted democracy only during the Depression, the majority of the elite (the civil service, the judiciary [courts and judges], the office corps, the academics and even the clergy) had rejected it virtually at birth.

Follow up more leads

At this stage in your enquiry, you will have a number of leads. You now need to follow them up, using the source file and any other useful sources you have found. Look back at page 44 to keep yourself on track. Review your material – can you identify any gaps which you need to research? What are the key areas that you should go into in more depth?

Review and organise material – reach conclusions

Finally, you will need to reach a conclusion. In this example you should identify the main reasons for the political problems faced by Weimar Germany in 1918–1923.

You could summarise your key points in a concept map like the one below.

- Impact of Treaty of Versailles
- Frequent changes of government
- Reasons for the Weimar Republic's political problems, 1918–23
- Left-wing unrest
- Right-wing unrest
- Government reactions to unrest

Enquiry and writing skills support

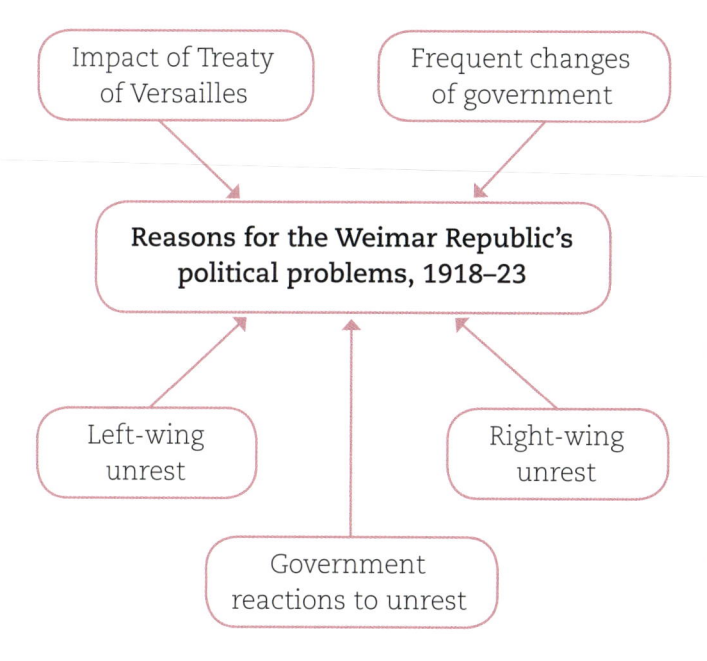

Draw extra arrows to show how the factors link, for example:

- outrage over Versailles linked to a distrust of the Weimar government and to political tensions
- government actions against extreme left-wing unrest had an impact on the influence of right-wing opposition.

Present your conclusions

The next two activities give you practice writing for your controlled assessment task. After you have completed the write up, you could turn to Maximise your marks on page 72 to see if your answer could be improved.

Activities

12. Make a set of notes to go with your concept map. Use the same headings. Do not use more than two sides of paper. You can include quotations from your sources in your notes. If you use them in your answer, make sure you explain why they are important.

13. Write up your enquiry: The reasons for the political problems facing the Weimar Republic in the years 1918–23.

ResultsPlus
Watch out

When you do your research, be careful not simply to copy things out – you should make notes in your own words and keep page references to show where you found the information.

ResultsPlus
Top Tip

You will get better marks for your Part A enquiry if you refer specifically to sources that you have read. For example, instead of saying 'some historians', include the actual name of the author. You can also use a short quotation.

Part A: Carry out a historical enquiry

Following up an enquiry 2: Changes in the role of women during 1933–39

This practice enquiry is different from enquiry 1, which asked you to find out about why the Weimar Republic's political problems developed. This enquiry gives you practice in making comparisons and deciding how much the role of women changed.

The Nazi regime had a strong vision of what the role of women in Germany should be, and it introduced different methods to make this vision into reality. However, the Nazi regime also had other priorities which didn't always fit with this vision, and there were practicalities to consider too – German agriculture relied on women workers, for example. So it is a very interesting topic for the historian: did women's roles change under the Nazis and, if so, to what extent and why?

Follow the enquiry stages outlined on page 44. Identify, sift and sort your information.

Begin by using pages 38–39 of this book. Then go on to the information given in the source file on page 51. You can follow up more leads if you like.

Don't forget to stick to the enquiry path when you follow up your leads, and remember the RDR tests (page 46). Because of the nature of the Nazi regime, we don't have many sources for what ordinary women really thought about their government. Most of the sources we have on this topic are from the regime itself, and are therefore not objective. However, historians have worked very hard over many years to establish reliable information about the role of women under the Nazi regime. Now you can benefit from all that work!

Activities

Making and sorting notes

Read pages 38–39 and the source file.

14. Make a bullet-point list of useful information, for example:

Women in Germany pre-1933
- Many women worked for a living (there were 10,000 women teachers for example)
- Women were starting to enjoy more freedom from traditional roles (e.g. make-up, fashion)

Nazi views
- Nazis thought women should not go out to work
- Role of women to raise children, look after house, care for husband
- No make-up or fashionable clothes

Nazi laws/awards
- Law for the Encouragement of Marriage (1933): loans to encourage marriage
- Mother's Cross award

Success for Nazi policies?
- Fewer women worked under the Nazis
- But the Nazis also needed women to make armaments: policy shift?

15. Begin to organise your notes. You could arrange them into a chart like the one below. This chart has been used to organise some statistics.

16. Now colour-code your chart. Use green to show similarities and red for differences.

17. Finally, think about how much change you can see. Give the chart a column heading: How much change in the years 1933–39? Fill this in and make sure you give reasons for your answers too.

Changes in the role of women 1933–39

Changes in employment – women in regular work
1925: 4.2 million
1936: 5.71 million
1939: 7.14 million
But: there were more jobs and more women of working age in the 1930s compared to 1920s.

Changes in marriage
1929: 589,000 marriages
1936: 609,000 marriages
1939: 772,000 marriages
By 1939, 42% of all marriages got a loan.

Changes in numbers of births
1931: 1 million
1933: 971,000
1936: 1.2 million
1939: 1.4 million

Enquiry and writing skills support

Source file

Source A: An extract from Edexcel *GCE History: From Kaiser to Führer: Germany, 1900-45*, Martin Collier, 2009.

> The first step taken by the regime to bring women into line with Nazi ideology was the creation of the Women's Front (*Frauenfront*) by Robert Ley on 10 May 1933. All 230 women's organisations in Germany were to expel their Jewish members and integrate into the Women's Front or face being disbanded. Most organisations happily obliged, pleased to support a regime they saw as nationalistic and supportive of the traditional role of women.

Source B: An extract from *A Social History of the Third Reich*, Richard Grunberger, 2005.

> Though there was much talk of forcing married women back into their home to provide jobs for men, this mainly affected the professions, and fluctuations in the female labour force were only marginal [i.e. there were only small changes in the numbers of women in work under the Nazis]. The truth was that female labour was cheaper: skilled women earned 66 per cent of men's wages, unskilled ones 70 per cent… Furthermore women workers were indispensable. In 1933 women formed 37 per cent of the total employed labour force in Germany. Every second agricultural worker was female; in addition, 75 per cent of female labour on the land was not hired but consisted of members of the family.

Source C: An extract from *Life in Germany*, Steve Waugh, 2009.

> There were successes. In the first few years the number of married women in employment fell. Moreover, the number of marriages increased and there was a rise in the birth rate…However, there were limitations and even failures. The rise in the birth rate may have been due to the economic recovery of the period rather than Nazi policies. Most couples continued to have families of two children.
>
> Moreover, the number of women in employment actually increased from 4.85 million in 1933 to 7.14 million six years later. From 1936, there was a labour shortage and the Nazis needed more workers in heavy industry because of rearmament.

Source D: An extract from a speech by Adolf Hitler to the NSDAP Women's Organisation (September, 1934).

> The slogan 'emancipation of women' was invented by Jewish intellectuals…If the man's world is said to be the State, his struggle, his readiness to devote his powers to the service of the community, then it may perhaps be said that the woman's is a smaller world. For her world is her husband, her family, her children, and her home. But what would become of the greater world if there were no one to tend and care for the smaller one?…This great world cannot survive if the smaller world is not stable…We do not consider it correct for the women to interfere in the world of the man…We consider it natural if these two worlds remain distinct.

Source E: An extract from *GCSE Modern World History*, Ben Walsh, 2001.

> There were some prominent women in Nazi Germany. Leni Riefenstahl was a high-profile film producer. Gertrude Scholz-Klink was head of the Nazi Women's Bureau, although she was excluded from any important discussions…Many working-class girls and women gained the chance to travel and meet new people through the Nazi women's organization. Overall, however, opportunities for women were limited. Married professional women were forced to give up their jobs and stay at home with their families, which many resented as a restriction on their freedom. Discrimination against women applicants for jobs was actually encouraged.

Source F: In *The Illustrated History of the Nazis* by Paul Roland, 2009, the caption to this photo reads: 'Hitler had a particular place in the hearts and minds of German women. Here, a party member watches rapt during one of his speeches. She is wearing Nazi insignia and "the mother's cross".'

Part A: Carry out a historical enquiry

Writing up your answer

The moderator will be looking for four main things – that you have:

- kept your answer focused on the enquiry
- found information from different sources
- backed up your statements with information
- communicated your answer by organising it well and using good spelling, punctuation and grammar.

The activities which follow will help you to improve your writing. Remember to use the skills you have learned when you write up your controlled assessment answer.

Activities

Improving writing

18. Study examples 1 and 2, imagining you are the moderator. Discuss with a partner the good and bad points of each example. You will find the answers at the bottom of page 53.

19. Suggest ways you could improve examples 1 and 2. You can do this in bullet point notes.

20. Study example 3. It is part of a high-level response. It compares roles, finding similarities and differences, and giving details. Now try adding to the answer by giving examples in each of the brackets. You can also add more paragraphs giving similarities and differences.

Did the role of women change between 1933 and 1939?

Example extract 1

> Under the Nazis the role of women changed from before because the Nazis wanted women to stop working and wearing make-up and they did.

Example extract 2

> The Nazis wanted women to stop working, to marry and to have children and the statistics show that marriages and birth rates both went up and that women were certainly forced to leave jobs for men to take them, especially in the early years of the Nazi regime. If marriages and birth rates had gone down then the policy would not have worked and if marriages had gone up but birth rates had gone down it would have been like a half success because there would have been more marriages like the Nazis wanted but not more babies which is what they thought was the role of women. And the same if birth rates had gone up but marriages had gone down because the Nazis thought women should have babies only when they were married. So the picture was quite different from life under the Weimar Republic, when women had started to break away from just being housewives and started to enjoy themselves in the night clubs of Berlin.

Enquiry and writing skills support

Example extract 3

The Nazi leaders were men and their view of women was very traditional. They did not think that women should go out to work or be involved in politics. Instead the Nazis thought that women should marry, look after their husband and raise their children so that Germany would have plenty of people. [Example gives quote from a speech by Hitler to support this point.]

Under the Weimar Republic, women had started to have more freedom from a traditional role of wife and mother. A lot of women had begun working for a living and many women had gone into professions like teaching or the civil service. Women had the vote under the Weimar Constitution. Although life in the countryside was probably much the same as ever for women, in the big cities a new world of fashion and good times was starting to open up for women.

The Nazis hated the changes in the role of women they had seen under Weimar. They used a variety of measures to make German women return to traditional roles. One of these was to order all women's organisations to become part of the Nazi Women's Front. They also used other methods [answer goes on to detail how the Nazis forced women out of professional jobs such as the civil service and explains, quoting sources, the Mother's Cross award scheme and the Law for the Encouragement of Marriage (1933)].

So on the surface it looks as though the Nazis really changed the role of women: away from freedom and back to Kinder, Küche, Kirche (children, kitchen, church). But actually historians have shown that the Nazis' policies did not achieve a complete change. First of all, there were some things that continued just as before. German agriculture depended on female labour before the Nazis and also during their regime. Then, there were changes like the big increase in marriages and the rise in the birth rate [answer gives statistical information backed by sources] although Steve Waugh says this was probably to do with improving economic conditions as much as Nazi policies. And the birth rate did not increase that much, so women were not having the huge families the Nazis had hoped for. Finally, women continued to work [answer supports this from sources], and in fact the Nazis had to change their policy and start encouraging women to work in the armaments industry.

Summary

Success in your enquiry comes from:
- sticking to the focus of the enquiry
- using a range of sources, keeping their relevance and reliability in mind
- organising your answer to show good quality of written communication.

Answers

Example 1 does identify differences, but it is not detailed enough and it does not identify any similarities. It does not refer to any sources.

Example 2 has more detail and has made some comments about similarity and difference. But the student has included a long discussion about what we can tell from birth and marriage rate statistics instead of looking at a larger range of examples. Also, there is not enough detail in the explanation, and example 2 does not refer to any sources.

Part B Representations of history

How were the Nazis able to control Germany 1933–39?

> **Learning outcomes**
>
> By the end of this chapter, you should be able to:
> - describe some of the problems historians have with studying life under the Nazis
> - describe some of the methods the Nazis used to persuade people to support them
> - understand the concept of *Volksgemeinschaft* (people's community) and explain why this was an attractive idea for many Germans.

In Part B of your controlled assessment you are exploring how the Nazis were able to control Germany through the 1930s. You have already seen in Part A some of the ways in which the Nazi dictatorship was set up and run. Part B builds on this information, but takes a different approach to how your knowledge is used.

A problem with the Nazis

Historians have a real problem with the Nazis. It is very difficult to discover what the German people in the 1930s really thought about them. The Nazi dictatorship dealt very harshly with Germans who were against the regime or who criticised it, so you can see the problem. If a German said they agreed with the Nazis, did they really mean it, or were they just saying that so they didn't get into trouble?

Another side of the problem is that a lot of the evidence that historians use comes from the Nazi regime itself. The Nazis controlled all media in Germany: newspapers, art, books, plays, radio, film. Since the Nazis wanted everything to show how successful their government was being, historians have to be very careful about using data from such sources.

This means it is not always possible to get definite answers to big questions like 'how were the Nazis able to control Germany?' Different historians use the available evidence in different ways to construct their representations of what happened. This can produce some very different theories!

A problem with us

Part B of this course relies on your skill in making an **interpretation**. You need to be able to look at a representation and work out what angle it is coming from, what point it is trying to express, what is missing from its depiction. What we know about the horrors of the Nazi regime make this a difficult task. We tend to look at representations of Nazi Germany as if we are wearing tinted glasses – coloured by what we know. Try the activity on the next page and see how this can work for you.

> **Context:** the situation, setting, circumstances and background which explain the meaning of an event.
>
> **Hindsight:** interpretation of the past using knowledge gained after the event.
>
> **Interpretation:** a view or explanation of the thing being examined.

> **Activity**
>
> 1. Imagine a historian of the future is studying life in your school. Give three reasons why this historian would have problems discovering how someone like you felt about your school rules.

How were the Nazis able to control Germany 1933–39?

Source A: A detail from *The Wool Collection at a Munich Local Group* by Adolf Reich, 1942.

Activity

2. Look carefully at the picture in Source A. What do you see? Which of these interpretations do you agree with:

   a) There are two Nazis in the picture – you can tell this because they have brown uniforms on.

   b) The two Nazis are demanding papers from people: this means the people are in trouble. Nazis ruled by fear.

   c) The old man and the old woman are probably Jews. They are frightened.

   d) There are piles of shoes: these are probably from other Jews sent to camps. There are piles of clothes – these are probably from Jews too.

   e) The picture shows ordinary German people donating clothes and shoes to help soldiers.

   f) Many of the people in the room would be Nazi Party members.

   g) The two officials are friendly figures: they are older men doing their best to cope with this mountain of generosity.

   h) Even a poor old couple are giving what they can for the good of Germany.

How did you do?

The artist intended to show e, f, g and h. It shows Nazi officials struggling to deal with the overwhelming generosity of ordinary Germans in this collection of clothes for charity. Is that what you saw when you first looked at the picture? Most people wouldn't. They'd see Nazis and imagine the picture is showing a, b, c and d.

So we must be wary of **hindsight** when using evidence. A good historian tries to understand **context**. This means using all relevant information you have about the period when you are interpreting a source. And it also means talking about what you don't know – like the problem of knowing what ordinary Germans actually felt about the Nazis at the time.

Part B: Representations of history

'Sticks and carrots'

There isn't one reason that explains why the Nazis were able to control Germany. There are lots of different factors involved. We can divide these into *sticks* and *carrots* – as in the two ways of getting a donkey to move: you can beat it with a stick, or you can tempt it with a carrot. Using the stick can be called '**repression**' of the people – forcing them to accept the Nazi rule. By offering the carrot, the Nazis also aimed to gain the people's **consent** to their control.

- The Nazis believed that it was right for the strong to dominate the weak. They were ruthless in punishing those who stepped out of line.
- The Nazis encouraged Germans to support the regime by promising more jobs, a higher standard of living, security, a strong Germany that the world would respect.

You will find representations from the period that involve both carrots and sticks – sometimes both at the same time! One issue for you is therefore to be able to recognise a carrot or a stick when you see it.

> **Repression:** when carried out by the state this means taking away people's freedom to make normal choices and decisions by using extreme and often violently forceful control.
>
> **Consent:** agreeing to or approving of something, often after thoughtful consideration.

Activities

3. Sort the cards on this page into sticks and carrots.
4. Which do you think would be the three most effective sticks, and which the three most tempting carrots?

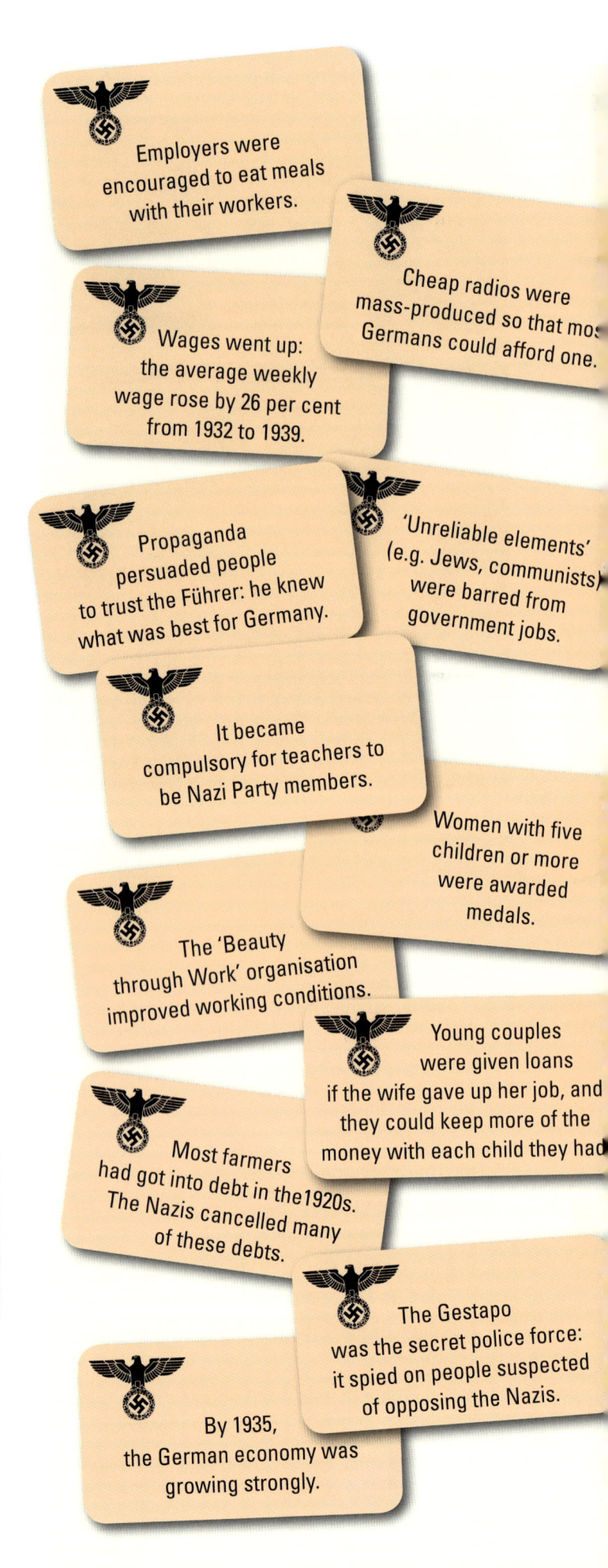

- Employers were encouraged to eat meals with their workers.
- Cheap radios were mass-produced so that most Germans could afford one.
- Wages went up: the average weekly wage rose by 26 per cent from 1932 to 1939.
- Propaganda persuaded people to trust the Führer: he knew what was best for Germany.
- 'Unreliable elements' (e.g. Jews, communists) were barred from government jobs.
- It became compulsory for teachers to be Nazi Party members.
- Women with five children or more were awarded medals.
- The 'Beauty through Work' organisation improved working conditions.
- Young couples were given loans if the wife gave up her job, and they could keep more of the money with each child they had.
- Most farmers had got into debt in the 1920s. The Nazis cancelled many of these debts.
- The Gestapo was the secret police force: it spied on people suspected of opposing the Nazis.
- By 1935, the German economy was growing strongly.

How were the Nazis able to control Germany 1933–39?

A massive employment programme reduced unemployment from 6 million people in 1933 to 0.5 million by 1939.

Young people were strongly encouraged to join the Hitler Youth (and it was compulsory by 1939).

'Undesirable elements' (e.g. political opponents of the Nazis) were sent to concentration camps; those who were released lived in terror of being sent back.

The 'Strength through Joy' organisation helped workers go on holiday and make the most of their leisure time.

Many new crimes now carried the death sentence – like telling a joke against the Nazis.

Joining the Nazi Party was a good way to get promoted at work.

By 1938, workers had the chance to save up to buy a car – unheard of at the start of the 1930s.

The SS could go into anyone's house at any time and could arrest people without trial.

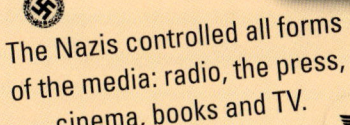

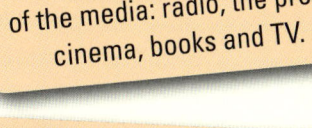

The Nazis controlled all forms of the media: radio, the press, cinema, books and TV.

Huge rallies were held to show German people how powerful and successful Germany was.

Censorship banned opinions or attitudes that the Nazis didn't agree with.

The Hitler Youth organisations had lots of exciting activities and were designed to make young people proud of the Nazis' achievements.

Activities

5. The Nazis collected lots of statistics, for example:

   - employment statistics
   - information on wages and the cost of different products
   - data on numbers of people getting married, age of marriage, number of children, etc.
   - Hitler Youth membership figures
   - information on industrial production
   - Nazi Party membership figures
   - crime data: numbers of people arrested for different types of offences.

   Which of the data sources listed above would you use to find out about the effects of the following 'carrots and sticks'?
   - Wages went up under the Nazis.
   - The Hitler Youth encouraged teenagers to become proud Nazis.
   - The Gestapo and SS punished anyone stepping out of line.

6. Choose another data source from the list and explain how you could use it to investigate another of your carrot or stick cards.

7. If you can find facts and figures about one of the Nazis' carrots or sticks, does that mean we can be sure we know the truth about how effective that carrot or that stick was? Why/Why not? (Hint: remember who was producing all this data.)

8. What problems do historians have when dealing with evidence about how the Nazis controlled Germany in the 1930s?

ResultsPlus
Top Tip

Films and television programmes can be very convincing. You will need to think about whether the situation and the attitudes shown in them fit in with your knowledge of Germany in the 1930s, for example, do they put too much emphasis on repression or on consent?

Part B: Representations of history

Dealing with propaganda

Some of the most interesting material from this period is Nazi propaganda. It is interesting because it is often very visual – posters, for example. But it is also a direct line to what the Nazis wanted Germans to do, what they wanted them to believe, how they wanted Germany to be. Nazi propaganda is packed with information about how the regime would have liked to control Germany. It's the historian's job to unpick the propaganda, measure it against what evidence we have, and make a judgment about what it tells us.

Volksgemeinschaft

You don't need to use German words in your controlled assessment but if you really did want to learn one word to impress your teacher, then *Volksgemeinschaft* would be the one! It is usually translated as 'people's community' and it had a very special meaning for the Nazi state.

Volk	+ Gemeinschaft
The German word *Volk* is the same as our word 'folk'. The Nazis were obsessed with the idea that the German people were very special.	*Gemeinschaft* means 'community' – a special sort of community, tied together strongly and rooted in its native land – like a brotherhood.

The Nazis were trying to create a *Volksgemeinschaft* in Germany: racially pure Germans, working together for the common good – a brotherhood rooted in German history. A lot of Nazi propaganda is built on this vision. It was designed to show off the benefits ('carrots') of the regime if you belonged to the *Volksgemeinschaft*. But Nazi propaganda also showed the dangers that threatened the community – and the need for a strong state that would defend (with 'sticks') the *Volk* against its enemies – communists and Jews in particular.

Activity

9. How do you think the *Volksgemeinschaft* concept helped the Nazis control Germany after 1933?

Source B: The slogan on the poster is 'Victory or **Bolshevism**'. 'Sieg' is the German word for 'Victory' and 'Bolschewismus' is the word for 'Bolshevism'.

Bolshevism: The political beliefs of the revolutionary Russian communists led by Lenin.

Activities

10. Decode Source B. What is the message that this poster is communicating?
11. How does it get that message across?
12. Do you think this poster did convince some Germans to obey the Nazis – 'for fear of something worse'?

German people in Nazi propaganda are not often shown smiling; instead they are full of a sort of stern joy. They are giving themselves up to Germany's great purpose. The German people are shown as healthy and fit – workers, strong from farm work or factory work. They are blond – racially pure. Families are the basic unit, with women shown as mothers. The posters portray everyone, including children, living in harmony because they are all living to serve the state.

Source C: This painting by Paul Padua is called *The Führer Speaks*. It was painted in 1939.

The point of this introductory section is to outline some of the issues that surround representations of Nazi control of Germany. Because of issues with evidence, historians have to weigh up all the different information available and make a judgment. So it is only natural that different historians have different views about this period. It doesn't mean that one historian is right and the other one wrong – most historians are skilled at research and at dealing with problematic sources. It means that there isn't any one right answer. That is an important point to keep in mind as you work through Part B.

Activities

13. Study Source C in detail. The family is listening to Hitler (the radio is on the shelf; Hitler's poster on the wall). What is the message of this painting? The artist has made deliberate choices about what has been included. Consider:
    - who is included in the picture
    - what sorts of jobs the people might do
    - why it is important that everything has stopped in family life.

14. What could a historian use from this picture as evidence of how the Nazis controlled Germany in the 1930s?

15. Is this painting a more useful source than the poster in Source B? Explain your answer. (Hint: think why the artist might have been painting this picture – can art be propaganda?)

Summary

- We know that the Nazi regime used a combination of carrots and sticks – repression and consent – to control Germany.
- But because of the brutal nature of this regime, we can never be sure whether Germans went along with the Nazis out of fear or because they wanted to – or because of some mixture of these.
- Historians can weigh up the evidence available, but there is not one correct answer to this important question.

Part B: Representations of history

Understanding and analysing representations of history

Learning outcomes

By the end of this topic, you should be able to:

- understand what is meant by representations of history
- understand how historical representations are created
- analyse representations and judge how far they differ from one another.

What are representations of history?

A representation is a depiction of the past either visually or in words. It is designed to create an image of things in the past – an event, a movement, the role of an individual and so on. Historians create representations when they write about the past. They construct for us a picture of what life was like, why people acted as they did, and what the consequences of events and developments were. Novelists, filmmakers and cartoonists also give us an image of past societies and events. In each case, the way they choose to show their subject creates a representation of it.

Analysing representations

Someone who creates a representation takes some of the same steps you might take when taking a photograph or creating a Facebook entry. You choose what you are taking a photograph of or how to show yourself. Do you want to record an important event? And do you want to show it as happy or solemn? Do you want to show the beauty of a particular place? To get the effect you want, you choose which things to focus on. Sometimes you decide to leave things out. In this way, you make decisions about how to portray the scene or the event.

When you analyse a representation you should look at each part separately and think about how it affects the overall image. From the details, you can infer (work out) what impression the artist or author is trying to give.

A modern example of a representation

Let's first take a modern example and use the same skills needed to analyse a historical representation. Study Source A.

Source A: An illustration from the website of the British Tourist Board, 2009. It shows a scene on the east coast of England.

Inclusion of the boat and the windmill.

Blue sky: would the photograph have been taken on a rainy day?

Uncrowded scene: no objects in the centre of the picture.

Happy-looking young couple: do people look happy all the time? Why has the photographer not shown just one person alone?

Understanding and analysing representations of history

Note the details the photographer has chosen to include. Why have these details been included? What messages are they designed to give? Can you suggest anything which may have been deliberately left out? What do you think is the purpose of the representation in Source A?

Now study Source B. It is a photograph taken in the middle of an August morning. It shows a part of the coast near to the place shown in Source A. The building in the background is a nuclear power station.

Source B: A holiday photograph taken at Sizewell on the Suffolk coast, August 2009.

What parts of Source A are supported by details in Source B? Would you use Source B to advertise holidays on the Suffolk coast? If not, why not? If so, what parts of the photograph would you select?

Source A is not *inaccurate*, but Source B helps to show us that Source A is not a *complete* representation. Source A is one view and, when we analyse it, we can infer the message and purpose of this representation from the choices the photographer has made. Source A is designed to portray the coast as attractive and uncrowded, a place to enjoy walks and be happy. Its purpose is to encourage people to take holidays in the area.

Activity

1. Describe the representation of the east coast of England given in Source A. Use details from Source A. You could begin 'Source A is a representation of the East Coast. It is designed to portray it as…We can tell this because…'

   Try to use most of the following words and phrases in your description. You can use them in any order:
   - selected
   - chosen to
   - omitted
   - deliberately
   - highlighted
   - included
   - incomplete.

   You can also use details from Source B if you wish.

Part B: Representations of history

Nazi propaganda and historical representations

The Nazi regime set out an attractive vision of a national community for the German people. Compared with the misery of unemployment and the shame of national defeat, the Nazis promised a strong nation, respected by the world, with good standards of living. And the Nazis did more than promise an attractive vision. Under Hitler, the economy did improve. Unemployment was reduced. Germany won respect in the world.

Underneath this bright, attractive vision, however, was repression, fear, brutality and murder. The Nazis never tried to hide the fact that the wonderful future was only for certain people. Others were excluded, for example the Jews, disabled people, Gypsies, homosexuals. Also, the Nazis protected the *Volksgemeinschaft* from political opposition, especially from communism. Anyone who did not conform to the regime would be excluded from it.

The role of propaganda

Propaganda was not as negative a term in the 1930s as it is now and the Nazis had a Ministry of Public Enlightenment and Propaganda, headed by Goebbels. He saw his role as telling the German people what the regime wanted them to do 'in such a way as they understand it'. As you saw on page 34, the regime had lots of different ways to get its message across: radio, cinema, sporting events, political campaigns. The Nazis used propaganda to create representations of the regime. As historians, we can analyse these representations to show the message or messages they contain. We can:

- identify what the Nazis wanted people to believe or feel
- weigh up those claims against our own knowledge
- examine what was left out of the message.

Case study: Standards of living and the North Sea holiday

Source C shows a poster advertising the North Sea resort of Norderney, an island off the North Sea coast of Germany. The image looks like a photograph but it is actually a 'photomontage': different photos put together plus added colours and graphic effects. It is a bit like using Photoshop today: image manipulation to create a particular effect. The poster is from 1937.

So, let's look at this poster in more detail.

- What message is it designed to get across?
- What other knowledge can we add to our analysis?
- What does it tell us about how the Nazis were able to control Germany?

Source C: A poster for the North Sea resort of Norderney, 1937. The text at the bottom of the poster reads: 'Seaside sunshine, sea breeze, seawater: the three main attractions of the North Sea coastline'.

Understanding and analysing representations of history

Face value

At face value, this is a typical advert for a seaside resort. People are shown having a good time. The sky is blue and cloudless. This blue colour has been added to the photo, and the colours have also been enhanced to make a more pleasant effect in other parts of the image.

Digging deeper

To our eyes the Nazi flags do not belong in a seaside holiday advert. They look completely out of place. But for historians, these flags make the image very interesting. This poster is advertising a Nazi holiday. What other Nazi symbols does the image use and how does it use them?

- The girls are blonde: Aryan.
- The girls are fit and healthy: they are active rather than sunbathing.
- The photo has been arranged so the girls frame the Nazi flags in the centre – the flags are the most important.
- The flags are not real: they have been added to the original photo – this is a 'photomontage'.
- The caption to the poster emphasises sun, sea and sea breezes. The message is: Nazi holidays = clean, healthy, bracing.

Adding your own knowledge

This is a poster for a holiday resort so it links to standards of living under the Nazis. Remember that one reason why the Nazis could control Germany was because they promised that German people would have a higher standard of living. Read more about this in the context box.

Context: the standard of living debate

Most people had suffered a lot from economic hardship in the 1920s and early 1930s. The Nazis created jobs to tackle unemployment, but they also made it possible for ordinary people to own more consumer goods, like radios, and to go on holiday.

The Strength through Joy (KdF) organisation was a massive part of working life under the Nazis. In 1934, 2.3 million people took KdF holidays; by 1938 it was 10.3 million.

Historians agree that the Nazis got a lot of support from ordinary people in this way. The Nazis did not just control Germany through fear. Those included in the *Volksgemeinschaft* also benefited from the regime.

However, there is a debate about whether the Nazis really did raise the standard of living, or whether the changes were just cosmetic (see page 41). For example, thousands of Germans saved up for a 'People's car', the *Volkswagen*. But no one ever received one this way, the scheme was cancelled when the war began.

What's missing?

With any Nazi propaganda you should always consider what is missing from the representation. For example, Source C is definitely advertising a German holiday for the racially pure. No Jews would be welcome. Also, anyone suspected by the regime of working against the *Volksgemeinschaft* would find it difficult to go on a Strength through Joy holiday. Only those in the national community could take part.

Activity

2. Write your own description of the representation in Source C. Remember to dig deep, connect it to your own knowledge and point out what is missing from the representation in order to show what message it has chosen to communicate.

ResultsPlus
Top Tip

Always use your own contextual knowledge to help you analyse a representation.

Part B: Representations of history

Analysing written historical representations

To analyse written representations, you can use the same skills you have already developed to analyse visual sources. You should note what the author has chosen to focus on, what he or she has chosen to include, what has been omitted, and how words are used to build up an impression. For example, in Source D the Nazi propaganda ministry presents the portrayal of the Nazi regime which it wishes newspapers to give.

Source D: The Nazis controlled all the newspapers. This is an extract from a press conference by the Ministry of Public Enlightenment and Propaganda, for newspaper editors.

> Photos showing members of the Reich Government at dining tables in front of rows of bottles must not be published in future, particularly since it is known that a large number of the Cabinet are abstemious [drink little]. Ministers take part in social events for reasons of international etiquette and for strictly official purposes, which they regard merely as a duty and not as a pleasure. Recently, because of a great number of photos, the utterly absurd impression has been created among the public that members of the Government are living it up. News pictures must therefore change in this respect.

Activities

3. How does Source D try to create a representation of the Nazi leadership? What does it focus on and what accusations does it reject?
4. What does this extract tell you about how the Nazis went about controlling Germany?
5. Does the fact that some Germans were laughing at pictures of drunken ministers mean the Nazis were controlling Germany, or not?

Analysing the views of historians

The views of historians are also representations. Historians writing about any society have to make choices. They choose what to concentrate on. They also come to views about the topics they research. Using the evidence, they make judgments about the role of individuals or the reasons for an event, and so on. In their writing, they give their views. Sometimes historians' views differ.

But we cannot think about historians' writings in quite the same way as we did for Sources C and D. Unlike representations like these sources, historians aim to create an accurate representation of the past that they have researched. The views of historians may differ because they're looking at or looking for different things, or because they interpret the evidence differently.

Activity

6. Study Sources E and F. They are written by historians. Which of the following statements are correct? You can choose as many as you like. (The answer is at the bottom of the page.)
   a. The historians disagree.
   b. The historians do not actually disagree.
   c. The historians are writing about different things.
   d. The historians are using different sources to analyse the impact of standard of living under the Nazi regime.
   e. Both historians' views about the impact of standard of living under the Nazi regime are accurate.

Answers

All answers except a are correct. The views are different, but they are not actually disagreeing with one another.

Understanding and analysing representations of history

Source E: An extract from *The Nazis: A Warning From History* by Laurence Rees, 2005.

> Erna Kranz was a teenager in the 1930s and is now a grandmother living just outside Munich. She remembers the early years of Nazi rule, around 1934, as offering a 'glimmer of hope…not just for the unemployed but for everybody because we all knew that we were downtrodden.' She looked at the effect of Nazi policies on her own family and approved: salaries increased and Germany seemed to have regained a sense of purpose…'I thought it was a good time. I liked it. We weren't living in affluence like today but there was order and discipline.'…. It is vital that people like Erna Kranz speak out, for without their testimony…[it might be thought] that the regime oppressed the German population from the very beginning. Academic research shows that Erna Kranz is not unusual in her rosy view of the regime during this period. Over 40 per cent of Germans questioned in a research project after the war said they remembered the 1930s as 'good times'.

Source F: An extract from *Life in Germany* by Steve Waugh, 2009.

> From 1936 to 1939 wages actually increased, but this was due to a longer working day rather than an increase in hourly wage rates. Average working hours in industry actually increased from 42.9 hours per week in 1933 to 47 hours per week six years later. In addition, the cost of living increased during the 1930s, which meant that real wages (what workers could buy) actually fell. All basic groceries cost more in 1939 than in 1933. There were also food shortages, because the government reduced agricultural production in order to keep up prices.

The differences between these two historians are explained by what they are looking at. Rees interviews people about their memories of the period while Waugh concentrates on statistical data. Rees's focus is on people's attitudes to the regime, while Waugh lets the data speak for itself. His focus is on the economic impact of the regime on people's standard of living.

Although they are different, both can be accurate in their views. Just as when people in a house look out of different windows, or look into the distance or close to the house, their different focus will give them a different view of the scenery. It will be important to keep this idea of focus in mind when you look at differences in the representations of historians. Historians are not usually wrong or inaccurate when they differ, but they may have looked at the topic from a different perspective.

ResultsPlus
Watch out

If historians disagree with one another, don't assume that one historian must be wrong. Think about what they are focusing on.

Comparing representations

Sources G and H (on the next page) are both about how the Nazis controlled Germany in the 1930s. How far do they differ? To find out, follow these three steps.

1. Analyse each source. When analysing representations you should identify the big points first. Historians usually make a big point – their main conclusion or view – and they use detail points of evidence to back it up. In Sources G and H, the main points have been highlighted.

2. Compare the sources. Make a table like the one which has been started on the next page, so you can compare the sources carefully. In the first column put specific points you want to check. In the second column add anything from the other source which supports or challenges this point. Use the third column to make notes on what you have found.

3. Reach a conclusion about 'how far'. Decide how much the differences you have found actually matter. Are they small differences, such as a matter of detail, or big differences about the main points of the representation? How much agreement is there? Weigh up the similarities and differences to decide how far they differ.

Part B: Representations of history

Activities

Create a table like the one on this page.

7. Identify points you want to check in Source G. Remember that you are looking at the question of how the Nazis controlled Germany. You could enter big points in red and smaller details in black or blue. The table has been started for you. How will you colour-code the points already there?

8. Check Source H to see what is said about these points – are they confirmed, challenged or just not mentioned?

9. Now repeat, starting with Source H and look for any extra points you've so far not compared.

10. Weigh up the differences and write your conclusion. Include these key phrases (delete the words which do not fit your conclusion):
    - There are some/many points on which the two sources agree…
    - However there are small/major differences in the way they explain why most ordinary Germans went along with the regime…
    - Overall they are mainly in agreement/differ to a large extent in their representations of the reasons why the Nazis could control Germany…

Source G: An extract from *Nazism 1919–1945* edited by J. Noakes and G. Pridham, 2000.

> While relatively few Germans were turned into committed Nazis, the overwhelming majority were reconciled [happy to go along] with a regime which satisfied many of their basic needs and… [agreed with] their basic values. Although terror… provided a crucial element in the stability of the regime [kept it strong], consent was an equally or even more important foundation for it.

Source H: An extract from *The Hitler Myth: Image and Reality in the Third Reich*, by Ian Kershaw, 1994.

> Frustration and disappointment with the realities of everyday life under National Socialism led ordinary Germans to grumble and complain, but seldom to… [show] 'resistance'. Why? Organised terror played a central role. But the most important [factor]… was Hitler's charismatic [appealing] leadership… [which] secured the loyalty to the regime of even those who opposed the Nazi movement itself. Millions of ordinary Germans believed that the Führer would certainly right all wrongs in Nazi Germany.

Points in Source G	Points in Source H	My notes
Relatively few Germans became Nazis.		Only around 10% of Germans joined the Nazi Party before 1939.
The regime met people's basic needs.	People did grumble and complain.	The Nazis did deal with unemployment – though in a short-term way.
The regime reflected most people's ideas.		Germany was already anti-Semitic before 1933.
Terror was a crucial element.	Terror had a central role.	Both sources agree.
Control was based on consent.	Control was based on loyalty to Hitler.	

Summary

- Representations of history are created to give an impression of an aspect of the past.
- The impression is created by what is included and by the way details are drawn, or by the words used.
- Historians' interpretations are also representations of the past. They sometimes differ because of the historians' focus.

Evaluating representations

When you are evaluating a representation, you are deciding how good it is. When you evaluate anything in everyday life – what clothes to buy, for example – you use **criteria**. Does it fit? Is it in fashion? Is it too expensive? Is the colour right for you? You also make some criteria more important than others. If something doesn't fit, you won't buy it, even if the colour is right!

You will also use criteria when you weigh up representations of history. But let's work on an everyday example first, and then you can apply your skills to evaluating historical representations.

Activity

1. With a partner pick a film or TV drama you have both seen.
   a) Choose three criteria by which to evaluate it, for example 'funny' or 'action-packed'.
   b) Give it a rating of 1–3 against each of the criteria, and discuss your rating with your partner. You do not need to agree, but you should each be able to back up the rating you give. Refer specifically to the film or drama.
   c) Give the programme or film an overall star rating of 1–5. Make a display to explain your overall evaluation to your class, making sure you refer to the criteria you have used. Was one criterion so important that it had the most influence on your overall rating?

Criteria: rules or tests on which judgements can be based.

Using criteria to evaluate representations of history

There are many different kinds of representation. You could be judging between an extract from a history book, a cartoon, a work of historical fiction or a film portrayal of an event in the past. Apply criteria to each of them to make your judgement. But remember, in order to weigh up a historical representation you must first have good knowledge of the issue which is represented.

Using your knowledge, you can apply these tests to a representation:

- Is it *accurate*? Test the representation against what you know. Is it correct?
- Is it *complete*? Does your knowledge suggest important aspects are missing?
- Is it *objective*? Analyse the representation to see whether it is fair or unbalanced in its treatment. Here you could also think about the purpose of the author or artist.

For example what overall star rating 1–5 would you give to Source A? It is a Nazi poster from 1936 portraying the Nazis' achievements in reducing unemployment.

Source A: A Nazi propaganda poster from 1936. The text reads: 'Before: Unemployment, Hopelessness, Neglect, Strikes, Lockouts. Today: Work, Joy, Order, National Camaraderie.'

Part B: Representations of history

First study the context box. Then follow the steps in Activities 2–4 to help you reach your judgement.

Context for Source A

- The Nazi regime did deal effectively with the major challenge of unemployment.
- Major work creation schemes were set up, such as building new roads.
- The RAD (see page 40) organised manual work for the unemployed.
- Trade unions were broken up and workers were paid according to how much work they did.
- The numbers of hours worked a day increased.
- Wage increases did not go up as much as the cost of living, so by the end of the 1930s wages were actually worth less than in 1933.
- Large numbers of unemployed men were drafted into the armed forces.
- Women were encouraged (through marriage loans and propaganda) to give up jobs to be housewives, creating jobs for men.
- Jews and political opponents of the Nazis were forced out of jobs, which were taken by others.

Activities

2. Draw up a chart in three columns headed: 'How accurate?', 'How complete?' and 'How objective?'.
3. Fill in your three columns for Source A. You can use points given in the context box and the poster and add points of your own.
4. Write notes for your overall evaluation of Source A. Make these bullet points rather than whole sentences.

ResultsPlus — Watch out

Never try to evaluate a representation without first making sure you know the context. You can only judge whether something is accurate, complete or objective if you have good knowledge of the subject yourself.

Evaluating representations created by historians

Historians aim to give you their view of past events. The details in their writings are likely to be accurate. But you will still need to think about whether the view they give is the best one, depending on what you want to find out. If you want a detailed view of a period in depth, then a historian looking at overviews is not the best one for you.

Look back at the activities on page 66. You saw that what shapes a historian's work is what the historian wants to explore and what they are choosing to focus on.

Even if two historians are both looking in depth or overview, they can still be looking for different things and so they can still have a different view. Think about this when you read Sources C, D and E.

How important was terror in explaining how the Nazis controlled Germany?

So far in Part B we have considered representations that deal mostly with the idea of consent: that the Nazis were able to offer enough 'carrots' to make the German people accept their control over Germany. But to what extent did people only go along with Nazi control because they feared terrible consequences if they stepped out of line?

What did people believe?

This is a difficult area for historians. We have the Nazis' own propaganda, which of course says that the German people were delighted to be living under the Nazi regime. But, as Source B says, we don't know what people really thought.

Evaluating representations

Source B: An extract from *Nazism 1919–1945*, edited by J. Noakes and G. Pridham, 2000.

> Not only were there no opinion polls but it was impossible for people to express their views in public with any freedom; the results of elections… were rigged; the media were strictly controlled. Newspapers are of limited value as a source, since the editors were subject to detailed instructions from the Propaganda Ministry on what to print and were severely disciplined if they stepped out of line. In short, an independent public opinion did not exist in the Third Reich.

Most adults in Germany would have known of someone who was forced out of their job because of their political beliefs, or because they were Jewish or married to a Jewish person, or were in some other way unsuitable. Many might also have known of someone sent to a concentration camp for 're-education', most of whom never returned as the 1930s went on. So we can be sure that most adults recognised that there were serious penalties for acting against the regime. A key question for historians is therefore:

- did people obey the Nazi regime out of fear
- or did they agree with the Nazis that threats to the *Volksgemeinschaft* (see page 58) had to be removed?

There are other possibilities too, for example did people put up with the Nazis for fear of something worse – like living under communist control? Or did people believe that Hitler would put everything right as soon as he found out about the bad ways in which the other Nazis were acting?

Historians' views

Historians have represented the Nazi police state in some different ways. At first, many people believed that the Nazis had controlled Germany through terror: especially through the Gestapo (the secret police), and the concentration camp system run by the SS.

More recently, some historians have pointed out that there were too few Gestapo officials to have this level of control over the whole of the German people. Although the Gestapo actively investigated those they thought were a real threat to the regime, ordinary people got into trouble not because the Gestapo was spying on them, but because their neighbours reported them to the police.

That makes for a significant difference in representations that you can look out for. Which of the following statements does a representation agree with – or is it somewhere in the middle?

a) People obeyed the Nazis because they feared the Gestapo would find out if they didn't.

b) Some people believed in the Nazi regime enough to inform against their neighbours – enough to lose someone their job, get them arrested, or maybe even sent to a concentration camp.

Source C: An extract from Jacques Delarue, *The History of the Gestapo*, 1964.

> Never before in no other land and at no other time, had an organisation attained such a comprehensive penetration [of society], possessed such power and reached such a degree of 'completeness' in its ability to arouse terror and horror, as well as in its actual effectiveness. [The Gestapo] spotted or overheard every German's slightest movement.'

Source D: An extract from *The Nazis: A Warning From History* by Laurence Rees, 2005.

> Like all modern policing systems, the Gestapo was only as good or bad as the cooperation it received – and the files reveal that it received a high level of cooperation…Only around 10 per cent of political crimes committed between 1933 and 1945 [in the Würzburg district] were actually discovered by the Gestapo; another 10 per cent of cases were passed on to the Gestapo by the regular police or the Nazi Party. That means that around 80 per cent of all political crime was discovered by ordinary citizens who turned the information over to the police or the Gestapo. The files also show that most of this unpaid cooperation came from people who were not members of the Nazi Party – they were 'ordinary' citizens.

Part B: Representations of history

Source E: An extract from *The Third Reich: A New History* by Michael Burleigh, 2000.

> Much of the modern literature on the Gestapo has conveyed the impression of desk-bound policemen, almost buried under the avalanche of denunciations from ordinary citizens, particularly regarding violations of racial legislation…[S]ome historians have claimed that there was no difference between Gestapo 'excesses' and those of policemen in America or Britain, [which]…is of course completely ridiculous. The Gestapo's primary task was to destroy political and clerical opposition. It was clearly highly effective, for the Communist underground was smashed in waves of arrests…

Activities

5. Copy this chart and complete it using as many of statements a–h as you choose. Write a statement in both columns if you think it belongs in both.

Delarue	Rees	Burleigh

Notes for my overall evaluation of the representations

a. The author's focus is on how the Gestapo operated.
b. The author's focus is on explaining why other historians have made mistakes about the Gestapo.
c. The author's view is that the Gestapo was in complete control of the population.
d. The author's view is that the Gestapo could only operate because ordinary Germans informed on each other.
e. The author's view is that the Gestapo was designed to detect and remove organised opposition, not to control ordinary people.
f. This is a good representation of how the Nazis were able to control Germany.
g. This representation, although accurate, is not complete because…
h. This representation does not include…

6. Create your own context box for these representations (Sources C, D and E). Add detail on:
   - how and why the Gestapo was set up
   - the relationship between the Gestapo and other parts of the Nazi police state (e.g. the courts, the secret services, the SS and concentration camps)
   - the types of people the Gestapo targeted.

   You can find more information on these points in Part A of this book, on pages 30–33. You can add more points to your chart if you wish.

7. Which is the best representation of the Gestapo's role in the Nazis' control of Germany, 1933–39? Produce a short oral statement or a PowerPoint presentation (to last about half a minute) to evaluate both representations, and give your judgement about which you think is better. Make your criteria clear.

ResultsPlus
Top Tip

Remember, two answers can come to different judgements and still get the same marks. The important thing is to be able to show that you have used criteria and can back up your decisions using the representations themselves and your own knowledge.

Nazi control – repression or consent?

There isn't one single, correct answer to the question 'How were the Nazis able to control Germany 1933–39?' As you have seen, historians can disagree even when looking at just a single area of study such as the role of the Gestapo.

So, for example, Rees and Burleigh (Sources D and E) are both writing accurately and objectively, but they give us different views of the relationship between the Gestapo and the 'ordinary' people of Nazi Germany. How can they have different views and yet both be accurate? They can because their focus is different.

- One historian wants to show how the Gestapo could not have exerted its control over Germany without the active cooperation of thousands of ordinary Germans – this is a broad focus.
- The other wants to narrow the focus: Burleigh argues that the Gestapo's primary role was to smash communist opposition, not to gain control over the lives of ordinary Germans.
- One historian (Rees) sees consent as a key factor: many ordinary Germans wanted to help the Gestapo, for whatever reason – and the Gestapo relied on them.
- The other historian (Burleigh) argues that repression was more important: the Nazis were determined to destroy their 'enemies', communists and Jews, and the Gestapo did that very effectively.

Although there isn't an answer everyone agrees on, at least we have some useful ways to approach evaluations:

- Is a representation accurate?
- Is a representation complete or does it leave something out?
- Is a representation objective or biased?
- What is the focus of a historian's representation (detail or overview, etc.)?
- What is the purpose of a historian's representation (what are they arguing)?

And we have useful ways to consider the question of how the Nazis controlled Germany in the period 1933–39:

- by repression – the Nazis stamped down on any sign of opposition
- by consent – the Nazis also offered the German people things they really wanted.

These points should come in useful as you work through your Part B representations. Remember also that the question of how the Nazis controlled Germany in the years 1933–39 is one of the most important questions there is. Since we don't know exactly why the Nazis were so successful, there is always the worry that it could happen again.

Evaluating representations

Activities

8. Why do you think the Nazis were able to control Germany during 1933–39? Could something similar ever happen in Britain? Explain your answer.

   In the 2008 film *Die Welle* (*The Wave*) a teacher tries explaining the Nazis' control over Germany by setting up a single community of students bound by strong discipline and exclusion of non-members. Bad things happen! You could watch this film (below) to help you think about whether a Nazi-style takeover could ever happen in Britain.

9. Complete questions B (i) and (ii). Then turn to Maximise your marks on page 72 to see if you need to improve your answer.

   B (i) Study Sources D and E on pages 69–70. They are both representations of how the Nazis were able to control Germany during 1933–39. How far do these representations differ? (10 marks)

   B (ii) Study Sources C, D and E on pages 69–70. Choose the one which you think is the best representation of how the Nazis were able to control Germany in the years 1933–39. Explain your choice. You should use all three representations and your own knowledge to explain your answer. (20 marks)

Summary

- A historian's writing will usually be accurate and objective.
- Criteria must always be used when evaluating representations.
- The criteria could be: the accuracy, comprehensiveness, objectivity and purpose or focus of the representation.

ResultsPlus
Maximise your marks

Part A Carry out a historical enquiry

In this task, you are required to carry out an enquiry; the enquiry focus will be set by Edexcel. The task is worth 20 marks and you should aim to spend about an hour writing it up. The mark scheme below shows how your work for this task will be marked. Remember that in this task you are also assessed on the quality of your written communication: use historical terminology where appropriate, organise the information clearly and coherently, and make sure your spelling, punctuation and grammar are accurate.

Level	Answers at this level…	Marks available
Level 1	Make simple comments. There are few links between the comments and few details are given. Only one or two sources have been used in the enquiry.	1–5 marks
Level 2	Make statements about the enquiry topic. Information is included that is mostly relevant and accurate, but it is not well organised to focus on the point of the enquiry. A range of sources has been consulted and information taken from them.	6–10 marks
Level 3	Are organised to focus mainly on the point of the enquiry. Accurate and relevant information is given to support the points the student makes. A range of sources has been found and well-chosen material taken from them.	11–15 marks
Level 4	Focus well on the point of the enquiry. A well-supported conclusion is reached, for example about: the nature of change OR whether one factor was more important than the others OR the inter-relationship between two or more of the factors (depending on the enquiry focus). A range of sources appropriate to the enquiry has been identified and material from the sources has been well deployed.	16–20 marks

Let's look at an extract from one student's response to the following enquiry:

- The reasons why the Weimar Republic faced political problems in the years 1919–23.

Student response

The Weimar government faced many political problems because they had to sign the Treaty of Versailles and most Germans hated it. It was very hard on Germany. Land was taken away and they had to pay reparations. German newspapers had cartoons which showed the allies to be like the devil. The government was weak and the Weimar Constitution made it hard to have a strong government. The Republic was soon under attack from both left- and right-wing extremists. The radical left accused it of betraying the workers' movement by preventing a communist revolution. Right-wing extremists opposed any democratic system. Extremists of the left and right hated the Weimar Republic. Reconciling themselves to it was unthinkable. What they hoped to do was destroy it. A big problem in 1923 was hyperinflation. Germany was poor and weak, and because they could not pay all the reparations from the Treaty of Versailles, France invaded part of Germany to take coal. There was hyperinflation and many people lost all their money. There are photographs from the time showing children playing with stacks of money and people using banknotes to light fires. People blamed the government. Because of all this Hitler led the Munich Putsch in 1923. It failed and he was put in prison – but not for long. The courts treated right-wing terrorism with a leniency best exemplified by Hitler's one-year jail sentence. Basically most of the problems came from the Treaty of Versailles.

ResultsPlus
Maximise your marks

Moderator comment

This extract indicates that the response would gain a mark in level 2.

The student has found out about and described the political problems facing Weimar Germany to 1923. The response shows the selection of some accurate detail. However the student's treatment of material is mainly descriptive and casual statements are underdeveloped. The student seems to have made use of a range of sources. It seems likely that the student has combined notes from different sources. However, the material has not been smoothly integrated and phrases have often been copied directly from text into notes and from notes into the response – using the words of the sources but not quoting from them. This means that the student cannot be given high marks in level 2 for quality of written communication.

To improve the response, the student should focus more centrally on the precise enquiry: the reasons for the political problems of the Weimar Republic. The student could show the linkage between the weakness of the Weimar Governments and:

- opposition from extreme left- and right-wing groups in Germany
- the impact of the Treaty of Versailles
- the problems of the constitution
- the lack of support from powerful groups.

Additionally, the material should be better organised in the student's own words rather than joined together from notes. Quotations should be acknowledged.

Let's look at an extract from an improved student response.

Improved student response

The period 1919-1923 is often called the 'years of crisis' for the Weimar Republic. It faced many political problems during this time, including serious attempts to bring the government down both from the left wing (the Spartacist Revolt) and from the right wing (the Kapp Putsch). My research into this enquiry suggests there were three main groups of problems. The biggest problem of them all was the Treaty of Versailles. After Germany had lost World War I, the victorious side had imposed strict punishments on Germany, designed to make sure Germany would not be able to go to war against the rest of Europe again. Part of the Treaty of Versailles was that Germany lost territory; part of it was that it had to massively reduce its armies and part of it was that it had to pay reparations to the winning side. [The answer uses sources to add details of the Versailles Treaty.] This was a political problem for Weimar because the German people hated and resented the treaty and many blamed members of the Weimar Republic for accepting it. Alan White says, 'The treaty provoked outrage within Germany – outrage which the extreme right was able to exploit for its own ends.' I think the Treaty of Versailles was the biggest reason for political problems in Germany in the years 1919-23 because most of the other problems Weimar faced came from it or were reinforced by it. A second group of problems related to the extreme right and the extreme left in German politics. Although the Weimar government had many socialists in it, the communists wanted a communist revolution in Germany and were frustrated that the government was blocking this. They launched the Spartacist Revolt to try and bring the revolution about. It failed because the government got the Freikorps, the extreme right-wing heavies, to put down the communists. But this caused further problems because it made the right wing stronger. The right wing of German politics hated everything about Weimar because of the 'stab in the back' theory. The Freikorps launched their own putsch, which the government subdued by calling on the communists to back a general strike. [The answer gives more details about the two revolts, using information from sources.]

ResultsPlus
Maximise your marks

> But right-wing extremists continued to be a problem. When hyperinflation developed in 1923, Hitler led the Munich Putsch, but the short jail sentence he received shows us why Weimar governments had such problems with the right wing. Richard Grunberger says, 'The courts treated right-wing terrorism with a leniency best exemplified by Hitler's one-year jail sentence...the majority of the elite (the civil service, the judiciary, the office corps, the academics and even the clergy) had rejected it [the Weimar democracy] virtually at birth.' A third main problem was caused by the way the government worked. The Weimar Constitution used a system of voting called proportional representation. This system meant that many smaller parties were elected and it was difficult to reach agreements, even on very serious issues. The government also changed very often, [answer gives details of the changes, quoting Richard Evans] and this meant it was hard to develop long-term approaches to problems. The weakness and instability of the government was caused by other problems too: it was unpopular because of Versailles; this made it hard for it to win the support of the German people, which made it harder to control the extreme left and right that threatened its existence.

Part B(i) Compare two representations

In this task, you are required to analyse and compare two representations of history. The task is worth 10 marks and you should aim to spend about 30 minutes writing it up. The mark scheme below shows how your work for this task will be marked.

Level	Answers at this level…	Marks available
Level 1	Identify the main features of the two representations by giving descriptions, direct quotations or paraphrases from one or both representations.	1–3 marks
Level 2	Identify the differences in two representations by comparing similarities and/or differences in their details.	4–7 marks
Level 3	Show understanding of the similarities and/or differences in the way the past is represented in the two extracts. The answer uses precisely selected detail from the two representations to support the explanations and the judgment about how far the representations differ.	8–10 marks

Let's look at an extract from one student's response.

- Study Sources D and E from pages 69–70. They are both representations of how the Nazis were able to control Germany in 1933–39. How far do these representations differ? (10 marks)

Student response

> Source D and Source E are both about the Gestapo. They both say that ordinary people gave information to the Gestapo. Source E does not agree with Source D about why the Gestapo was effective. Source E says the Gestapo was effective because it smashed the communist underground. But Source D says the Gestapo was effective because all the ordinary Germans helped it to discover political crime. So overall they are very different.

Moderator comment

In this part of the answer, the student shows understanding of some details in the representations and does compare them. We can see the language of comparison is used: 'Both about...', 'does not agree', 'are very different'.

The student is aware of differences between the sources, but does not bring them out explicitly: Burleigh directly criticises the view that the Gestapo relied heavily on ordinary Germans denouncing their neighbours (which would support a 'consent over repression' point of view). He uses exaggeration to indicate his challenge to this view: 'buried under an avalanche...'.

There is enough comprehension and comparison for the answer to get into level 2, but to raise the response to the next level, the answer should show more awareness of the extent of difference in what the two sources are portraying. The student could do more to unpick the difference and provide evidence (such as quotes from the representations) to back up the arguments. The student could also have discussed more than one difference or similarity between the representations. For example, both representations agree that the Gestapo was effective (though they disagree on how this effectiveness came about); both refer to modern police systems (though in different ways) and, significantly, they disagree about the key issue of consent or repression, with Rees implying a much higher level of consent.

Let's look at an improved version of this answer.

Extract from an improved student response

Source D and Source E are both about the Gestapo and the role it had in controlling Germany under the Nazis. Both of the sources agree that the Gestapo was effective, although Source E does this more clearly than Source D. Both also compare the Gestapo to modern police forces (though in very different ways)... But they disagree completely about how the Gestapo was effective.

Source D argues that the Gestapo was only able to track down 'political criminals' because ordinary Germans gave them their names. This implies that most 'ordinary citizens' agreed with the regime and with the Gestapo, and were happy to help get rid of anyone suspected of acting against the Nazis.

Source E is completely opposed to this idea. It criticises historians who see the Gestapo as 'buried under the avalanche of denunciations from ordinary citizens'. Instead, it says the Gestapo was focused on destroying underground communist and church opposition. It says it was effective at this because communist opposition was smashed. Source E does not think that what ordinary Germans did is very relevant to how the Gestapo helped secure control.

So, overall they are very different. While Source D says the Gestapo were effective only because of consent from ordinary Germans, Source E says they were effective because of their repression of organised opposition to the regime. This is a big difference. Moreover, Source E directly criticises the view contained in Source D of the importance of cooperation of ordinary Germans with the Nazis.

ResultsPlus
Maximise your marks

Part B(ii) Analyse and evaluate three representations

In this task, you are required to analyse and evaluate three representations of history. The task is worth 20 marks and you should aim to spend about an hour writing it up. The mark scheme below shows how your work for this task will be marked. Remember that in this task you are also assessed on the quality of your written communication: use historical terminology where appropriate, organise the information clearly and coherently, and make sure your spelling, punctuation and grammar are accurate.

Level	Answers at this level…	Marks available
Level 1	Show some understanding of the main features of the sources and select material. Simple judgments are made about the representation, and a limited amount of accurate information about the period is given. The material is not detailed; links between the information and the representation are not explicit.	1–5 marks
Level 2	Show an understanding of the main features of the three sources and select key features of the representations from them. Judgment is made about the best representation and detailed and accurate information about the period is added. There is little linkage between description and judgment. Judgments may relate to the accuracy or comprehensiveness of the representation.	6–10 marks
Level 3	Analyse the three sources and show some of the ways in which the past situation has been represented. Detail from the sources is used to support the analysis. There is a critical evaluation of each representation based on well selected information about the period and at least two clear criteria are applied, for example, the author's purpose or objectivity, or the accuracy, comprehensiveness of the representation.	11–15 marks
Level 4	Analyse the three sources to show the way in which the past situation has been represented. Precisely selected detail from the sources is used to support the analysis. There is a critical evaluation of the representation based on precisely selected information about the period and applying at least three criteria, for example the author's purposes or objectivity, or the comprehensiveness and/or accuracy of the representation.	16–20 marks

Let's look at an extract from one student's response.

- Study Sources C, D and E from pages 69–70.

Choose the one which you think is the best representation of how the Nazis were able to control Germany in the years 1933–39. Explain your choice. You should use all three representations and your own knowledge to explain your answer. (20 marks)

Student response

I think Source D is the best because it uses accurate data not just words or views. But it doesn't say why people helped the Gestapo. But then no one agrees on that anyway.

I think Source C is useful because it does say how the Nazis were able to control Germany – because of terror. I think that is true too. Both Sources C and D are better than Source E in explaining Nazi control.

I think Source E is not so useful because it just goes on about other opinions of historians being ridiculous. That is not respectful of the other historians. It is maybe biased against the other historians by saying this, which means it is not so useful as a representation.

ResultsPlus
Maximise your marks

Moderator comment

The student has made a short comment which identifies some core information which each representation can provide.

The student has begun to use some criteria to evaluate the representations, but none of the comments are developed very far. The student uses the criterion of accuracy to evaluate Source D. This is a good choice of a criterion by which to evaluate these representations, as the other two offer no evidence at all for these claims (in the extracts provided). But the student does not make it clear why Source D's data is more accurate than the representations in Sources C and E. To improve the answer, the student should make more use of contextual knowledge and demonstrate what accuracy means in this context.

In evaluating Source E, the student has chosen the criterion of bias. Although the source does make strong criticisms of other historians, the charge of bias seems too strong here. It would have been better for the student to have discussed differences in the views and focuses of the three sources, and to have gone into some depth to justify his or her conclusions and explain the context for his or her own evaluation, relating the evaluation to what the student knows to be significant about the way the Nazi regime controlled Germany in this period.

To reach the highest level the student must also make use of more criteria – three should be used to rate each representation.

Let's look at extracts from an improved student response.

Extract from an improved student response

I think Source D is the best because it provides the most balanced, accurate and objective representation of the way the Gestapo fitted into Nazi control of Germany in 1933-39. I also agree with the view Source D sets out: its conclusion that ordinary Germans identified with the regime enough to inform on their neighbours fits well with my own knowledge about consent and repression under the Third Reich.

Source D is based on the research into specific records. Although the Gestapo destroyed most of their records at the end of the war, we know that the records for the city of Würzburg in Germany survived and that there were far too few Gestapo agents to have controlled the city's population. We also know most of the 'political crimes' the Gestapo dealt with (e.g. about mixing with Jews) were reported to the Gestapo or police by members of the public. Source D draws strong conclusions from this evidence: that many 'ordinary citizens' were very happy to cooperate with the regime. This view implies that the Nazi regime would not have been able to control Germany without consent from the German people.

Because Source D is based on the evidence of Würzburg it seems to be more accurate and objective than the other two sources. Sources C and E do not give any evidence of any kind (in the extracts chosen) for their claims. Source C represents the 'traditional' view of the Gestapo. At the end of the war, the view was that the German people had obeyed the Nazis, even helped them with the genocide of the Jews in the Holocaust, because they were too scared to resist them. When historians interviewed Germans who had lived under the Nazis, most people gave this explanation. But although it is very understandable, historians should not just go on what people say. They should research the facts and examine all available data carefully. Otherwise they will not be as accurate and objective as possible. And as Source D shows, the evidence we have from the Gestapo themselves suggests that not all Germans simply obeyed Nazi orders. Many of them actively helped the Nazi regime hunt down and destroy people suspected of acting against the Volksgemeinschaft...

ResultsPlus
Maximise your marks

Source E directly criticises the view that the Gestapo were only really effective when helped by the public. Instead, Source E says that the Gestapo was a very effective organisation for smashing organised communist and church opposition. This suggests that the Nazis were able to control Germany mainly because they brutally searched out and destroyed any real opposition to their regime. In this view, it doesn't really matter whether ordinary people informed on each other or not. Without any organised opposition, ordinary people had no chance of standing up against the regime and knew very well what would happen to them if they did.

Source E does not provide any evidence for its claim in this extract, which makes it less easy to say how accurate it might be. The remarks it makes about other historians making 'ridiculous' claims also makes you wonder whether Burleigh is more interested in picking a fight than in being objective. While Source D is making a particular argument — that ordinary Germans cooperated with the Nazis — it backs that up with evidence. In contrast, Source E seems to be creating an exaggerated picture of what other historians have said about the Gestapo just in order to knock it down. Like Source C, it doesn't deal with evidence about cooperation, but while Source C was written before this evidence was available, Source E knows about it but rejects it because it doesn't fit with Burleigh's argument.

Source D is reporting a new kind of view about the Gestapo, in contrast to the old picture we had (like Source C gives) — a one-sided view of a rule of terror that does not mention cooperation at all. It is trying to balance the picture we have of the Gestapo with what real evidence actually says. In doing that it misses out other aspects of what the Gestapo did. But I do not think that Source E is more balanced than Source D because we know that there was a high level of public denunciations. That means that while the Gestapo may have been smashing any organised opposition, and while these actions might have been very high profile and influential, the vast bulk of their time was spent following up on reports from one German against another. If the ordinary German people had chosen not to help the Gestapo, if they had protected those acting against 'racial legislation' (which I guess means dealing with Jews) instead of reporting them, even if they had just done nothing rather than actively cooperated with the Nazis, then the Nazi regime would have found it far harder to control Germany.

For these reasons: accuracy, objectivity and balance, I conclude that Source D is the best representation of how the Nazis were able to control Germany in 1933–39. It shows that the Nazis ruled with a mixture of consent and repression. They could never have got to the level of control they achieved without the German people's active help and support.

Glossary

Allies: the countries fighting against Germany in the First World War – originally Britain, France and Russia.

Anti-Semitism: hostility towards or prejudice against Jews.

Autarky: being self-sufficient; for example economic policies which try to make sure that a country does not have to rely upon other states for vital goods.

Bolshevism: the political beliefs of the revolutionary Russian communists led by Lenin.

Censorship: banning views or information which you do not want people to see.

Consent: agreeing to or approving of something, often after thoughtful consideration.

Constitution: the rules for governing the country.

Context: the situation, setting, circumstances and background which explain the meaning of an event.

Criteria: rules or tests on which judgements can be based.

Dictatorship: a state governed by one person who has total control.

Gemeinschaft: Gemeinschaft means 'community' – a special sort of community, tied together strongly and rooted in its native land – like a brotherhood.

Great Depression: the period after 1929 when much of the world suffered from a decline in industries, agriculture and trade.

Hindsight: interpretation of the past using knowledge gained after the event.

Inflation: a general increase in prices; this means that money buys less – it loses its value.

Interpretation: a view or explanation of the thing being examined.

One-party state: a state where only one political party is allowed to govern.

Persecution: systematic mistreatment of an individual or group of people.

Plebiscite: a public vote.

Police state: a state in which the government uses the police – sometimes secret police – to control people's lives.

Propaganda: information or ideas used to influence people's attitudes and beliefs.

Putsch: German word for rebellion or revolt.

Reich: a German word used to signify the German state or German nation.

Reparations: money paid by Germany to repay the Allies for their losses in the First World War.

Repression: when carried out by the state this means taking away people's freedom to make normal choices and decisions by using extreme and often violently forceful control.

Volk: the German word Volk is the same as our word 'folk'. The Nazis were obsessed with the idea that the German people were very special.

Published by Pearson Education Limited, a company incorporated in England and Wales, having its registered office at Edinburgh Gate, Harlow, Essex, CM20 2JE. Registered company number: 872828

Edexcel is a registered trademark of Edexcel Limited

Text © Pearson Education Limited

The rights of John Child and Rob Bircher have been asserted by them in accordance with the Copyright, Designs and Patents Act 1988.

First published 2010

12 11 10
10 9 8 7 6 5 4 3 2 1

British Library Cataloguing in Publication Data
A catalogue record for this book is available from the British Library.

ISBN 978 1 846908 78 1

Copyright notice

All rights reserved. No part of this publication may be reproduced in any form or by any means (including photocopying or storing it in any medium by electronic means and whether or not transiently or incidentally to some other use of this publication) without the written permission of the copyright owner, except in accordance with the provisions of the Copyright, Designs and Patents Act 1988 or under the terms of a licence issued by the Copyright Licensing Agency, Saffron House, 6–10 Kirby Street, London EC1N 8TS (www.cla.co.uk). Applications for the copyright owner's written permission should be addressed to the publisher.

Designed and typeset by Juice Creative Ltd, Hertfordshire
Original illustrations © Pearson Education Ltd 2010
Printed in Great Britain at Scotprint, Haddington

Picture credits

The publisher would like to thank the following for their kind permission to reproduce their photographs:

(Key: b-bottom; c-centre; l-left; r-right; t-top)

akg-images Ltd: 5, 8, 13, 16, 29; **Alamy Images:** Paul Mathias Padua 59; **BPK:** 39; **Bridgeman Art Library Ltd:** 'What does Spartacus want?' Spartacist League poster (colour litho), German School, (20th century) / Kunstgewerbe Museum, Zurich, Switzerland / Archives Charmet 9, The Last Blow! 1933 (colour litho), German School, (20th century) / Private Collection / Peter Newark Pictures 32, Caricature of Goebbels, 1938 (colour litho), Berman, Sam (b.1906) / Private Collection / Peter Newark Historical Pictures 34, Hitler's SS troops parade with Nazi standards on Party Day at Nuremberg, 1933 (colour litho), German School, (20th century) / Private Collection / Peter Newark Military Pictures 21, League of German girls poster, c.1935 (colour litho), German School, (20th century) / Private Collection / Peter Newark Military Pictures 37; **Bundesarchiv (Federal Archives):** o.Ang Plak 003-003-025 67; **CAS Department / Calvin College:** Adolf Reich 55; **Corbis:** 22, 36, 42; **Mary Evans Picture Library:** 51, 58; **Daily Express:** Sidney 'George' Strube, British Cartoon Archive, www.cartoons.ac.uk 27; **Getty Images:** Three Lions 7; **Imperial War Museum:** Breidenstein 62; **Kobal Collection Ltd:** RAT PACK FILMPRODUKTION 71; **Angela Leonard:** 61; **Photolibrary.com:** Rod Edwards / Britain on View 60; **TopFoto:** 2006 31, Punch Limited 25, ullsteinbild 15, 18, ullsteinbild 15, 18, IMAGNO / Thomas Sessler Verlag 15/2, 40

Cover images: *Front:* **Corbis:** Bettmann

All other images © Pearson Education

Every effort has been made to trace the copyright holders and we apologise in advance for any unintentional omissions. We would be pleased to insert the appropriate acknowledgement in any subsequent edition of this publication.

Websites

The websites used in this book were correct and up to date at the time of publication. It is essential for tutors to preview each website before using it in class so as to ensure that the URL is still accurate, relevant and appropriate. We suggest that tutors bookmark useful websites and consider enabling students to access them through the school/college intranet.

Disclaimer

This material has been published on behalf of Edexcel and offers high-quality support for the delivery of Edexcel qualifications. This does not mean that the material is essential to achieve any Edexcel qualification, nor does it mean that it is the only suitable material available to support any Edexcel qualification. Edexcel material will not be used verbatim in setting any Edexcel examination or assessment. Any resource lists produced by Edexcel shall include this and other appropriate resources.

Copies of official specifications for all Edexcel qualifications may be found on the Edexcel website: www.edexcel.com